Table Layout and Decoration

Audrey

WARD LOCK LIMITED·LONDON

© Audrey Ellis 1978

First published in Great Britain in 1978
by Ward Lock Limited, 8 Clifford Street,
London W1X 1RB, an Egmont Company

Reprinted 1982, 1986

Text filmset in 11 on 12pt Monophoto Baskerville
by Servis Filmsetting Limited, Manchester.

Printed in Great Britain by Hollen Street Press Ltd,
Slough, Berks.

British Library Cataloguing in Publication Data

Ellis. Audrey
   Table layout and decoration
   1 Table setting and decoration
   1. Title
   642.6   TX877

ISBN 0 7063 5415 X

Contents

Acknowledgements
The publishers and author would like to thank the following for kindness
and co-operation in supplying pictures and relevant material for this book:

BRONZEPLAN LIMITED (p. 87) cutlery, goblets, corn-on-cob sticks,
  salt and pepper set
GEORGE BUTLER OF SHEFFIELD LIMITED (p. 18) cutlery; (p. 69)
  teaspoons; (jacket) cutlery
DENBY TABLEWARE LIMITED (p. 17) tableware and cutlery; (p. 35)
  tableware cutlery, glass and furniture; (p. 36) cutlery
FLOWERS AND PLANTS COUNCIL (pp. 17, 18, 35, 36, 69, 70, 87,
  jacket) Flowerphone information service: Tel. 01-499 4191
KIWI PRODUCTS UK LIMITED (p. 87)
OLD BLEACH LTD (pp. 17, 18, 35, 36, 69, 87 and jacket)
PASTA INFORMATION CENTRE (p. 70)
PRICE'S CANDLES (pp. 35, 70, jacket)
RAVENHEAD GLASS CO. (jacket) 'Elegance' glasses
SELFRIDGES LIMITED (p. 35) candles, candlesticks by Ultima Tulle,
  sauce boat by Old Hall; (p. 36) 'Fox Hunting Scenes' tray, Boden mini
  vase; (p. 69) goblets by Arthur Price; (p. 70) teak salad bowl, green
  Melaware, salt and pepper set, French loaf tray, glasses by Italia, place
  settings by Viners; (p. 87) place settings; (jacket) butter dish
SINGAPORE ORCHIDS (p. 87)
R & C VINTERS (pp. 18, 35, 69)
WEDGWOOD LIMITED (p. 36) tableware; (p. 69) tableware; (p. 87)
  tableware; (jacket) tableware
JEREMY WHITAKER (p. 88) Photograph by kind permission of Lord
Hertford
Thanks also to Kimberley Clark, makers of Kleenex tissues

Introduction

A beautiful and appropriate table layout sets the scene for an enjoyable meal. With a little expertise in tablecraft you can create attractive colour schemes and harmonizing flower arrangements for any occasion. But you also need the right furniture and table accessories which, like an artist, you use as a medium to express your ideas and make the perfect background for the food.

These are items to choose with care. Few of us possess several complete sets of china, sideboards overburdened with cutlery and suites of glasses, or even a linen cupboard full of different table-cloths and napkins. The dining-table and chairs usually have to serve any purpose, from simple family meals to the most elaborate dinner parties.

When you shop for dining room furniture and table accessories it pays to have a general plan in mind for the kind of life you lead both in terms of daily eating and entertaining your friends. Originality adds spice to the art of table setting. Study also how to mix and match your prized tableware to present different, original layouts whenever you wish. Before you buy anything new always consider its potential; many tempting items could easily run away with your budget and yet would not have a multi-purpose use.

Everything you buy for the service of food, other than pieces which are purely ornamental and decorative, should be chosen to give excellent long-term wear. Cutlery, glass and china must be easy to wash and restore to sparkling freshness every time. (There is, of course, very good disposable tableware for parties and this should not be overlooked.) Spills and smears are impossible to avoid. Table surfaces that are simple to keep in perfect order and cloths that can be trusted to come up like new after dozens of launderings are splendid friends to the housewife, especially if she is often also a hostess. So knowledge of how to choose and care for every item from the all-important dining-table down to the last teaspoon is invaluable.

The one ingredient we need never be short of, in creating all sorts of lovely table settings, is imagination. This book is planned to give the basic information that will help you to give your own imagination free rein and adventure successfully with this fascinating craft.

Part 1
How to create
co-ordinated table layouts

Household possessions are often expensive investments. This chapter is to help you avoid the pitfalls of choosing unwisely and therefore making a bad investment, even in minor matters. Impulse buys are often at fault; why acquire a set of coloured glasses which are badly balanced and all too easy to knock over, or which distort the colour of drinks unpleasantly? By learning to spend a little time and thought before you spend your money, you are more likely to be satisfied with your purchases, and to find pleasure in using them.

TABLES

An attractively set table need not be a valuable antique or a masterpiece of modern design. If it is the right height, with space to give enough elbow room for the people who gather round it to sit comfortably, it can always be dressed to give a welcoming impression and need not look the same every day. Sometimes the surface can be covered with a cloth, or partially covered with place-mats. Your table setting can be simple or elaborate, informal or elegantly formal in turn. The shape of the table is important, and also the size and placing of legs, because these considerations govern the way it is set, and how many people can be accommodated. Have in mind the number who will usually be present at mealtimes and the largest number you might reasonably want to seat for special occasions. Can you manage with a table which will not extend, or must it be adaptable with gate legs or extra leaves to be fitted in when required? Would you prefer your table to be large enough for buffet parties? These are some of the questions you should ask yourself when searching for the ideal table.

Size and shape

Whether choosing antique or modern furniture, decide calmly and not on impulse. If you haunt auctions and second-hand shops hoping to pick up an old table that is really worth what you pay for it, or wait patiently until the sales come around at a good furniture shop, have in mind exactly what you are looking for. It is so easy to be seduced into buying a beauty which is not quite suitable for your needs. Furniture always looks smaller in the shop than it does at home so have a plan of your room on squared paper (one square equalling 1m/3ft) with you when shopping. Measure the table and sketch it on to your plan to show how much space it will occupy. Consider too the size and shape of your dining room or the dining area set apart in an open-plan living room. Massive furniture tends to overwhelm a small room and delicate ornamental pieces look insignificant in a large one. Ideally each person needs 60cm/24in of table edge, 75cm/29in of table depth and 25–30cm/10–12in between the chair seat and the table top.

Suit the room

A dining room or dining area should never look overcrowded.

Round table A small square room might best be suited by a round table, because of the contrast in shape. The table itself need not be very large. Chairs can be placed fairly close together to seat guests. Some round tables can become ovals if fitted with a central leaf.

Oval table This shape suits almost any shape of room, and the table can probably be extended to become an elongated oval by adding a leaf. Again, shape contrast is given to a room which is not completely square by introducing pleasantly curved lines.

Oblong table The reproduction Jacobean or refectory table looks well in a room large enough to give plenty of space between the chairs and the walls; otherwise the impression is of an oblong within an oblong producing an unpleasing geometric pattern.

Where space is limited and the number you can seat all-important, remember that tables change shape when leaves are inserted or gate-leg-supported flaps raised. Check how the supports stand because the position of extra legs on the latter type of table can make seating cramped. The refectory table provides a maximum surface area for a minimum of legs (usually one central support running the entire length or simply a leg at each corner). Generally speaking, look for a table which does not exactly echo the shape of the room.

Most old dining-tables are large, or capable of being extended. A table with leaves of the separate or turnover type that swing into place as you pull the ends apart, will probably cost more than a fixed table top. Generally, antique dining-tables were constructed to seat large families and several guests, to support great weights of food and to remain steady as a rock; but do not be hasty in choosing a Victorian drop-leaf table. Many of the old drop-leaf type had pull-out legs on which the surfaces stood firmly when in use but these were intended for tea only. If strongly built, such small tables are not liable to collapse when loaded, and do very well today as dining-tables. They have the advantage of occupying only a minimal floor space when not set for a meal. (Even modern versions need to be looked at very carefully, to make sure they will stand the weight of food and china.)

Let us suppose your taste runs to an antique table with its satin sheen surface of mahogany or rosewood acquired through many years of faithful polishing. If it is of a useful size, stands firmly, and the legs are well positioned; such a table in perfect condition will probably fetch a high price. But sometimes an excellent old table can be acquired cheaply, if it has been defaced or damaged. If this can be hidden by the use of mats for individual settings and the lovely undamaged surface left exposed to collect the compliments which are its due, you might do well to buy it. If the damage consists of scratches and grooves, these can be filled, though not concealed, and you will always have to use table-mats. But do not be tempted by such a table if, for instance, the damage is right in the centre or near one corner, because it is bound to show.

Having dealt with the antique and second-hand table, or an attract-ive marked-down table in a store, let us turn to the purchase which should have no concealed dangers: the well known manufacturers' current popular design which you will order and have delivered to you possibly from the factory via the retailer's warehouse.

Shop around, scan magazines and send for manufacturers' cata-logues before you buy. Unless you are an expert, go to a reputable dealer. Most modern tables are made for modern families and seat four normally, and eight at the most. Can the table easily be extended? Is the design functional and in a style you can live with for many years, or will it date? Occasionally a short-lived fashion is painfully obvious a few years later and you wish you had never fallen for its transient charm.

Find out exactly what the table is made of. Is it solid wood, or a veneer and chipboard, or even a plastic laminate? You can tell solid wood, which incidentally might also be veneered with a more expensive wood, by looking for end-grain at the table edge. Check also for the latest sign of the real thing, the 'Touch Wood' swing ticket. Check the workmanship: look underneath for bad joints, rough finishing, loose screws, blobs of glue and finally at the overall finish. Get the manu-facturer's advice on the care of the table, how to preserve the pristine surface, and whether it is unwise to put it anywhere near a central heating unit or fire. (New wood often takes less kindly to temperature changes than old.)

Making do with what you have

Special occasions that overstretch your normal seating and table space only happen a few times a year in most households. If you have to supplement your non-extendable four-seater with a card table at one end, make a larger fit-on top to go over the dining table. Use 19mm/¾in chipboard – the supplier will cut it into shape. Clip it securely to the existing table with wooden swivel clips and add extra slip-in legs made from 25mm/1in dowelling to either side for added stability. Do cover your own table first with a protective cloth to prevent scratching.

Table lighting

The right kind of lighting can make or mar the look of a table, but many novel and ingenious effects are possible with electric lights and/or candles. Do you intend to place a centre light over the table? Or do you plan to have wall-sconces and no centre light? The fitting which can be raised or lowered over the table centre is much the most convenient, and can be fixed for most occasions at the height at which it conveys most harmony to the shape of the room and gives the best light; usually about 75cm/30in above the table. Choose a shade that sheds a diffused light, as direct lighting can be too harsh. You may like to fit an electric dimmer switch on the wall, to give more or less light to suit the occasion. Big lamps on the sideboard give an angled light. However pretty they may look before you sit down, this light is not very practical because the diners will sit between it and the food, casting shadows over the table. Some direct lighting on or over the table is therefore essential.

CHAIRS

Your dining-table naturally governs the style of chair you choose to go with it. It may well be that your table and chairs come as a matching suite, in which case the problem of choice is solved. Or is it? It is not satisfactory to buy a table which seems to you at the time quite perfect, unless the accompanying chairs are comfortable and suit the space available. If your dining area is part of an open-plan living room, make sure the upright chairs which will stand round the table are in tune with the armchairs and sofa. Traditional chintz covers might not live happily with ultra-modern black vinyl and tubular steel.

How many chairs

The size of your table, fully extended if it has leaves, will determine the number of chairs you can actually get round it. It would be a pity to buy a table large enough for big parties and then undermine its usefulness by choosing enormously wide chairs. Very narrow chairs are equally impractical. A seat of about 90cm/35in square is a good average size.

Seat heights will also vary to suit the height of the table: be sure to allow plenty of leg room.

Four dining chairs make up a basic set, but as time passes this number can become too few. When you buy, always check with the shop whether the style and pattern are a standard line and repeatable for some time to come and that chairs may be bought individually. If there is any doubt, you may prefer to choose again – remember a sale bargain may just be the end of that range. (Some second-hand chairs you will never be able to match, but they may blend in well with a classic style which is always available.) If possible, buy six chairs, rather than four. You can always tuck the extra ones away in a bedroom or in the hall if you are short of space in the dining room.

Choose for comfort

Make sure that your new chairs really are built strongly enough for people to sit on, and that they do not groan or rock precariously. It is a good test to sit on a chair, rocking it on to the back legs. Ominous creaks are a sign that it may not wear well. Sit on one of the chairs for several minutes, preferably pulled up to a table. Is it comfortable and does it offer the type of support you need? Ideally the top edge of a chair back should fit just below your shoulder blades. Some people like a solid back or slats, others prefer a partial or fully-open back with just a single support slat. Do you want chairs with arm rests? Dining-chairs with arms are called 'carvers' and are usually placed at each end of the table. It is common practice to have two 'carvers', for the host and hostess, with four plain chairs in the same basic style. 'Carvers' are not wholly practical with circular tables as they take up rather a lot of elbow room.

Styles of chair

If your dining suite is antique or 'reproduction' it will relate to one of several main periods of furniture design. The austere heavy styles in oak are Tudor or early Jacobean. Later Jacobean styles featured decorative scrolls on oak and walnut. Gradually other woods and fine wood veneers were introduced, and the use of gilding, oriental cane and lacquer. Furniture of this period was quite delicate. The heavy cabriole legs and broad seats of Queen Anne style are again distinctive, followed by finer designs in mahogany, walnut, satinwood and rosewood by Georgian craftsmen. Victorian furniture tends to be both heavy and ornate, a style which dominated fashion until the advent of

'Art Nouveau', still highly stylised but smaller, lighter and more suited to modern homes. Perhaps most of all in tune with today's lifestyle is the 'good honest furniture' created by William Morris and Ambrose Heal.

TABLE-CLOTHS

With a rainbow of colours, both printed and plain, to choose from you can frequently vary your choice of table linen. As well as being decorative, table-cloths also have a very practical purpose in protecting a cherished table top from the spots and spills which almost every meal brings. Most of these can easily be removed, but unless the surface is totally stain- and heat-resistant, constant cleaning which is not really good for the table top will be necessary – and disasters do happen! Covering your table with a cloth at least for mealtimes, saves the surface at the expense of washing the cloth, and most hostesses find this well worth while. The popular blends of terylene and linen, and polyester and cotton, give you all the qualities of the natural fibre, plus the easy-care of the man-made fibre.

Permanent table covers As we have said earlier, there are pretty tables of a shape and size to suit your dining room and your family needs, which have damaged tops not really worthy of display. Since it is now fashionable as well as practical, you may choose to put on a permanent cover over which a smaller clean cloth can be laid. Choice of style and material are matters for the expression of your own creative talent. Chenille is now enjoying a revival, in rich, intense colours. Make it frankly Victorian with a bobbled edge. Buy this edging by the metre and sew it firmly to the hem. Alternatively, make the cloth more tailored with a plain hem or braid border. The border weights the material and helps it to hang well. Cloths like this should reach, almost, or right to, the floor. Another alternative is to buy heat-resistant padding material, also available by the metre, which can be cut to fit the top of any table exactly, so that mats need not be used. The thinnest and least conspicious is a material called Bulgomme made of rubber. It has a surface which looks rather like linen and although it is only about 5mm/$\frac{1}{4}$in thick, it gives as good protection as the average heat-resisting mat. The great advantage is that you can cut shapes exactly to fit the top of your table or to place under mats which are not themselves heat-proof.

Green baize is an elegent choice, even when uncovered and looks striking with a well-polished oil lamp or sturdy plant in a decorated Victorian style of china or plain white plastic holder. A strong, vibrant shade of green might be the key to the whole décor of the dining room. Felt now also comes in many shades, but is not guaranteed to wash without fading or stretching, and even when dry-cleaned tends to stretch unevenly, creating puckers and a wavy edge. A few rows of machine-stitching round the edges with a loose tension helps.

Washable table-cloths If your taste is towards the formal, the snowy Victorian damask cloth is now produced in a terylene version, and in delicate pastel shades as well, with matching napkins. The cloths are available in sensible sizes for modern family tables. The pastels are particularly beautiful if covered with see-through Nottingham lace bought by the metre or as a finished cloth. At the other end of the scale of permanency, throw-away checked bistro cloths come in a sort of light-weight felted fabric, durable enough to survive laundering a few times. Although not heat-proof or even heat-resistant, the wipe-clean printed fabrics with a coating of vinyl are so much prettier than the old 'American cloth' associated with dreary, institutional table settings. Between the two, the choice is bewildering. The traditional woven cloth is easy to care for, both in natural and man-made fibres. The vinyl-coated cloths are literally drip-dry, the terylene ones, nearly so. Seersucker cloths require no ironing, merely gently pulling into shape as they dry and nylon seersucker actually looks after itself.

Making your own table-cloths

If you have a sewing-machine, or time to enjoy working by hand and embroidery, you can create table-cloths which cost much less than bought ones. A good department store will often sell terylene-cotton sheeting by the metre with simple, stylized motifs in various colours on a white background. They will also stock the same material with the motif reduced to half size. You could easily run up a beautiful table-cloth and a set of napkins in the scaled-down pattern, to match. Mail-order firms will send patterns of polyester and cotton easy-care sheeting in both strong colours and pastels, and in co-ordinated printed sheeting. The choice is yours – plain cloth and printed napkins, or the reverse. This enables you to mix and match your table layouts very easily.

The co-ordinated look may even go as far as matching a table-cloth to your curtain material. Many housewives make their own curtains but it does not seem to occur to them to make table-cloths.

Opposite You can use the same china for an informal lunch, shown here, or for a more sophisticated dinner, shown overleaf.

NAPKINS

In the days when napkins were always made to match the cloth there was little opportunity to create exciting designs other than by folding the material elaborately into fancy shapes. Today, napkins tend to be smaller and quite frequently contrast with the cloth so that the effect is achieved with a few simple folds. If you try to copy a complicated method of folding napkins illustrated in an old book you may find the result disappointing, perhaps because the napkin is not large enough and the material has too little body.

A large napkin, preferably starched, and at least 40cm/15in square is needed, whereas nowadays napkins are usually made only 35cm/13in square or less. Also, the material must be a true square and it is surprising how often you find a new napkin, when unfolded, is badly cut, or puckered by faulty edge-stitching. Before you buy a set of napkins, unfold them all and make sure you are getting a perfect set.

Folding napkins decoratively

To use small napkins for informal table layouts, here are some ideas for simple yet effective ways to embellish your setting. The easiest method is to fold the napkin in four to make a smaller square and then across diagonally to make a triangle. Or you can fold the napkin in half and then three times, concertina fashion, to place on a side plate.

Eight classic ways to fold napkins for formal occasions

candle

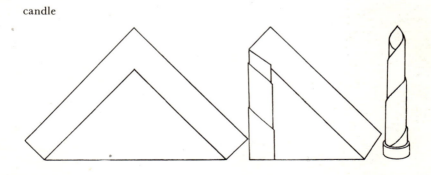

Left A thoughtful flower arrangement lends elegance to simple surroundings.

19

fan

lily

shell

butterfly

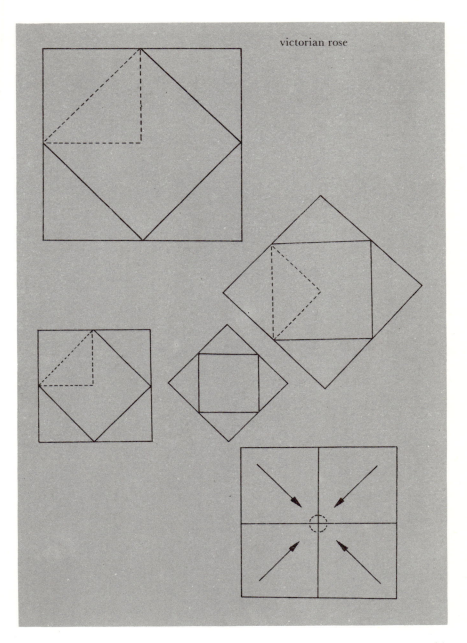

lady's slipper

mitre

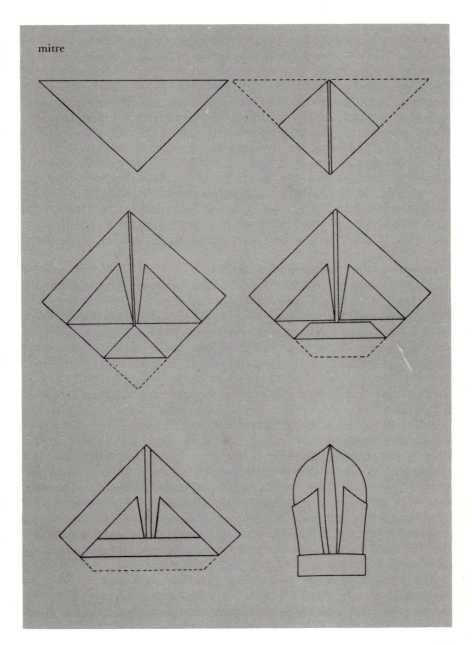

replacements too for the inevitable damage or disappearance of just one mat from the set.

CHINA

The ranges, patterns and types of china that are available today are truly marvellous. Not all of it is in fact 'china' although this generic term is used to describe widely different materials such as porcelain and earthenware pottery. There are ranges to suit all tastes and pockets. Fine china is made of a special clay; porcelain, which is sometimes almost translucent, and bone china which has the addition of bone ash to make it stronger. In most households porcelain or bone china is kept for entertaining and some form of earthenware used every day. Here are the main types you can buy and some observations on each.

Porcelain and bone china

This is the very best china you can buy for your table and, properly treated, it will last a lifetime. Its extremely delicate appearance is deceptive for it is very robust and unless knocked quite hard is far more resistent to chipping than one might think. Bone china is meant to be heated gently and should not be put into a very hot oven to warm, or in time the glazing will develop tiny cracks and the beautiful lustre will disappear. China decorated with gold or silver leaf is very expensive and requires extremely careful treatment. For example, the precious metal decoration could easily be damaged in a dish washer or a microwave oven.

If you like to serve food on very hot plates then a good toughened pottery or oven-proof glassware is perhaps a wiser choice. Even for the most important dinner party, a stoneware surface with a beautiful pattern can be truly elegant.

Neither china nor earthenware should come in contact with direct heat such as a low gas flame.

Pottery (Earthenware and Stoneware)

Within this category there is a wide price range because simple unglazed earthenware dishes are understandably much cheaper than oven-proof stoneware. Unglazed pottery is porous, dries out unless presoaked when exposed to extreme heat in the oven, and is liable to crack. Glazed earthenware is more durable but the most hard-wearing form is stoneware, equally suitable for use in the oven and for serving food on the table. Some earthenware has an underglaze pattern which makes it extremely pretty for daily use and at first glance might be mistaken for china.

Oven-proof glass

Specially toughened oven-proof glass goes happily from the oven to the table. In the right setting it can look very attractive when transparent and is also available in cheerful patterns on an opaque, pearly-white background. Oven-proof ceramic dishes have the added bonus that they can be taken straight from the freezer and placed in the oven or over direct heat. Care must be taken with oven-proof glass not to put a hot vessel or plate on a cold surface, especially if it is wet.

Another material for simple meal settings is the plastic now used to make very eye-catching ranges in Melamine, but the colours tend to be rather too intense to suit all tastes. If you like a strong grassy green, or brilliant sunflower yellow, without relief or adornment, you may enjoy using them. They need careful washing as stains do tend to build up on this material after repeated usage.

Choosing your china

Many of the points made here also apply to glassware.

When choosing your china, you must decide whether you wish to collect one particular design or if you are going to buy on impulse and change again when that particular service has been depleted by breakages. Both schemes have their advantages and a happy compromise might be to use a less expensive, easily replaced china for everyday meals and to use your more expensive china for special occasions.

If you are starting to collect a service of china make certain you choose a pattern that can be repeated when you want or can afford to buy more. The 'famous name' manufacturers will keep a pattern available for a great many years, but check carefully all the same. Sometimes you have to wait months until the manufacturer is repeating your particular pattern. One reasonably inexpensive way to acquire good china is to buy 'seconds'. These are frequently offered at sale time or can be purchased from the manufacturer's factory shop and it is well worth paying a visit to one of these shops if you are in the area of a leading pottery. If you do buy 'seconds' – usually at at least a third of the price or less of perfect goods – it is better to choose pieces with pattern flaws rather than misshapen ones, as these can rock on the table and cause accidents. It should also be noted that 'seconds' can constitute a stock clearance of discontinued ranges, in which case replacement pieces will never be available.

Finding exactly the right dishes

Among the 'special' pieces of china and pottery you might like to acquire are sets of dishes for specific items. Here are some I would recommend.

Artichoke plates: Round dishes embossed with a raised design of artichoke leaves, have a circular depression in the centre for the artichoke itself, and a dimple for melted butter or French dressing.

Avocado dishes: These come in exactly the right shape to hold half an avocado, either in chunky glass or fine bone china embossed with leaves.

Corn-on-the-cob dishes: White china holders which are fashioned in the shape of the leafy cradle in which the ear of corn lies; or nubbly shallow pottery platters, the right shape and size and printed with an embossed pattern of corn kernels.

Snail plates: Round metal, china, or pottery dishes (the latter with green speckles on white), made with dimples to hold from six to twelve snails. Escargots are not to everyone's taste, but these dimpled dishes are delightful.

Oyster plates: Round bone china dishes with shell-shaped indentations to take six oysters, and a dimple for a sharp sauce in the centre. Those in pottery have a 'woven basket' effect embossed round the shell shapes on the plates.

artichoke dish

avocado dish

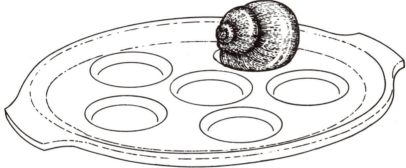

escargot dish

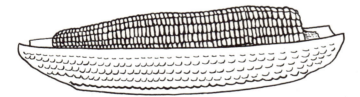

corn-on-the-cob dish

oyster plate in basketweave texture

31

CUTLERY

The price of cutlery varies enormously, according to the material it is made from and the quality of the finish. At the lowest end of the scale is stainless steel cutlery, although this rises in price depending on the quality of the steel and the degree of workmanship. Next comes cutlery made of stainless steel with wood, bone, china or stoneware handles. Silver-plated cutlery follows with the price again dependent on the thickness of the plate and the workmanship involved. Few people today can afford solid silver cutlery, so silver plate, especially Sheffield plate (which is silver-plated copper) is a perfectly acceptable alternative. A beautiful revival from the past is cutlery made of pewter. The new pewter is a much improved version, containing no lead (which used to be a health hazard, and also caused blackening). The eating parts are made of stainless steel and the cutlery can safely be put in the dish washer. The handles may be silver-plated, or finished simply with the soft, subtle glow of pewter. In either case, any tarnishing may be removed easily with a good silver polish. The revival of another ancient metal to table setting is bronze. Solid bronze is not only beautiful, adding a touch of luxury to your table with its unusual amber sheen, it is also as easy to care for as silver. Top of the price list and outside most people's budgets is gold-dipped stainless steel.

Before you make your choice, spare some thought for the time you can afford to spend keeping your cutlery clean. By far the easiest to care for is stainless steel. This good-tempered metal will stand up to almost anything and will withstand constant cleaning in the dish washer. Unless it is badly stained it needs no special cleaning or polishing. No other cutlery can be washed safely in a dish washer, and in fact, bone or wood handles may be totally spoiled by prolonged immersion in water. In fact, if you are unwilling to wash it very carefully, holding the handles of the cutlery out of the water, then a set made entirely of metal is your only sensible choice.

Size and pattern

Cutlery is made in an enormous range of styles and sizes. The decision on style is, of course, a matter for your individual taste and is probably governed by what will match the rest of the tableware you have or hope to acquire. Size has more practical considerations. Choose a style that will sit comfortably in your hand. Hold and feel the cutlery before you buy. Do you find the balance acceptable and do the handle ends fit comfortably into your palms or rest on your fingers? For this reason it is well worth buying your cutlery from a store that carries a wide selection. If you have young children do see that they are not expected to use cutlery that is far too big for their tiny hands. Invest in some special children's cutlery, or give them the smaller cheese and sweet knives and forks from your own range. Or even buy some cheaper stainless steel in a small size.

Quantities

If you are short of funds then you can cope initially with a knife, fork and spoon apiece. In such circumstances it makes good sense to buy a repeatable pattern and build up your stock gradually. The leading British manufacturers sell cutlery in full canteens for 6 or 12 or more place settings, or in individual place settings and some designs in individual pieces. These are the most desirable of all. You can also buy six special knives and forks in a set.

A typical place setting comprises the following pieces: meat knife, butter/cheese/dessert knife, meat fork, dessert fork, soup spoon, dessert spoon and teaspoon. If you make a practice of serving starters other than soup, you may need extra cutlery such as small pointed grapefruit spoons. Melon is eaten with a small knife and fork or a spoon and fork if preferred and hors d'oeuvres with a small fork only. A set of pearl-handled or unusual cutlery, co-ordinated with, but not matching everything else, may be the answer here. The fork can double at teatime for eating pastries in place of conventional pastry forks. The knife-and-fork approach is fine if people are sitting down at a tea-table. A cake plate balanced on the lap calls for a pastry fork only. Many canteens and place settings include teaspoons and coffee spoons, but not all. Proper coffee spoons are very much smaller because after-dinner coffee is traditionally served in small cups.

Condiment sets

Enclosed condiment sets with holes in the top of the shaker are designed to take pre-ground salt and pepper. Peppercorns and salt crystals which give a more pronounced flavour must be used in special mills. Do not expect your mills, which are usually made of wood, (and which may range in size from small to some 30cm/12in tall) to last forever. The grinding blades do become blunt and cannot be resharpened. In the interests of economy it is better to buy mills of good quality. On really formal occasions ground salt may be placed in a small salt dish. These are about 5cm/2in in diameter and often made of glass. The salt is transferred to the side of the plate with a small silver spoon – like a mustard spoon – but with a slightly longer handle. Mustard is also served in a small container with a spoon and may be sold with salt- and pepper-pots as part of a matching set.

GLASSWARE

There are three kinds of glass you might use on your table, and you probably have all three in your home.

Lead crystal

The most expensive hand-made glass which contains lead oxide. Because of its high light refraction it displays the contents to the finest advantage, and lends itself best to decorative cutting. Within this section there are several grades, so enquire carefully from the retailer the exact description of the high-quality glass to guide you on price.

The highest quality contains about 30% lead oxide and is distinguished by the name, 'Full Lead Crystal'. The next highest grade is 'Lead Crystal', containing slightly less lead oxide; the third grade is 'Lead Glass'. The higher the lead content the heavier the glass. All such glassware is brilliantly clear, relatively heavy, and will ring with a resonant tone when tapped. This is the table glass you will probably keep for parties only. It can be embellished with various decorations, principally by cutting and engraving. Deep cutting in elaborate patterns produces the most brilliant effect but is, naturally, the most expensive. Intaglio cutting is lighter, and therefore less costly. Beautiful effects are also produced by engraving with a copper wheel or stylus, but the result is more subtle than the bright sparkle of cut glass. The two methods can actually be combined in the same piece.

Soda glass

Moderately priced glass made from soda ash and silica sand can nevertheless be of very high quality. It can be hand blown but is more frequently machine-made. It is more often pressed than cut, and if so, the edges are not as sharp as lead glass, and the light refraction is not as good. ˊ

Opposite Your finest glasses, and tall tapered candles, complete the setting for a special dinner party.

Many people like to keep their cherished hand-made lead glass for special occasions, and use machine-made glass for every day. The latest designs in soda glass are elegant, but still functional and robust. It is particularly suited to the chunky modern designs many people prefer today.

Baked-on designs in colour make cheap glass cheerful but the colour of the pattern restricts the choice of table décor. It is useful to have plain cloths and napkins either to match or to make a pleasant contrast. Glassware without surface decoration may have 'bubbles', 'tears' and other patterns enclosed inside the glass and this form of design is becoming increasingly popular.

Heat-resistant glass

This really comes under the heading of oven-to-tableware and is more comprehensively described under 'Ovenproof glass' (see page 29), but it is also used to make glasses and cups for serving hot drinks and punches. Such glasses often come complete with holders to protect the hands. Bought holders are made of metal, plastic or raffia.

Deciding factors in your choice of glassware

Sometimes beautiful lead crystal glass seems expensive but remember that you may want to add to your suite of glass over the years to come, and you will want to feel certain that the pattern will be available when you can afford to add to your stock. This is a privilege worth paying for. If you admire some unusual display of glass (especially the cheaper imported type) in a store, take the precaution before you buy of enquiring whether the pattern is repeatable and whether you can rely on subsequent deliveries being an exact match. Sometimes the sizes or patterns of later batches are not quite the same. If not, buy a large supply while the going is good!

Some glass makers, such as Caithness Glass, are able to offer a very special service – having your glasses etched with a monogram or motif and perhaps even a design of your own choice. As with cutlery and linen, the personal touch of a monogram vanished with the growing expense of engraving and embroidering to order, but it seems now to show signs of reviving.

Top left Floating candles are a charming novelty and enhance a table setting.

Left A single flower makes all the difference to a breakfast tray.

wine   sherry   port   champagne

claret   liqueur   cocktail

brandy   highball   whisky

     Shapes of drinking glasses

Shapes of drinking glasses

Formerly a full suite of glasses would contain anything from ten to twenty different shapes. Nowadays we make do with far fewer and the rules are less rigid. Glasses for wine and spirits should be clear and reasonably fine, to display the colour to advantage. A wine glass should be two-thirds full; this allows an alcoholic drink to release its aroma – an important part of the pleasure of drinking.

Wine

The short-stemmed goblet is intended for red wines, so that your hand can naturally encircle the glass, so warming it. Claret glasses are tulip shaped, to retain the bouquet. Burgundies on the other hand are best drunk from wider glasses of the shape known as the Paris goblet.

White wines are served chilled in long-stemmed glasses. This is so that the hand only touches the stem and does not inadvertantly warm the wine. A champagne glass should be a tulip or flute shape to conserve the sparkle. Flat shallow saucer shapes do not improve this wine, but are nonetheless fun to drink from and perfect for champagne cocktails. Holding less than a tulip glass, they are ideal to sip from for a 'toast' on festive occasions.

Sherry and port

These glasses come in various shapes, but should have a smaller capacity than a wine glass. The copita or small tulip shape, half-full, is most suitable for enjoying the aroma and taste of sherry to the full. Glasses for port, Madeira and other fortified wines are not quite as tall as sherry glasses.

Liqueurs

Liqueur glasses are tiny as the quantity served is small. Many shapes are available, the most usual being like a miniature claret glass. A large liqueur glass can be used for brandy, but most men prefer a balloon glass which allows the warmth of the hand to release the aroma.

Other glasses

Whisky connoisseurs like straight-sided tumblers. Neat vodka and other 'national' spirits are served in small, slim, conical glasses with no distinct stems. Cocktail glasses are of a wider conical shape with a definite stem as cocktails are often served chilled or with crushed ice. American highball glasses are traditionally tall and straight-sided. Popular 'mixed' drinks – gin and tonic and the like – should also be served in highball glasses: as with champagne flutes, the tall slim shape helps to conserve the bubbles of the mineral. Beer is served in a large goblet or tankard.

Decanters and carafes
Decanters look magnificent on a table and are usually stoppered to prevent loss of bouquet from fine old red wines. Spirit decanters may be very simple in shape and elegant but are more often made from deeply etched glass. Since they frequently come in pairs, silver tags round the necks are not an affectation but are really necessary to identify the contents. The same can be said for decanters holding fortified wines (sherry, port, Madeira). The young robust red wines, taking the place of the classic clarets and burgundies now so expensive, do not have distinguished labels on the bottles. Since they benefit from prolonged exposure to the air to breathe, why not serve them *en carafe*?

Coloured glass and metal goblets
The fine lead crystal glass we take for granted today has only been widely available for the last 200 years. It reveals the quality and often the beauty of the wine which certainly cannot be fully appreciated if served in coloured glass or metal goblets. Nevertheless, the latter add a kingly touch to the table. Colour was often used to disguise imperfections in the glass and there is still some inexpensive and beautiful glass which adds intense colour, such as rich green or amber, to a table setting. The only problem is that these distort the colour of the drink. For this reason warm colours such as amber, golden yellow and tawny pink are 'kinder' than green or blue.

CANDLES AND HOLDERS

Once a necessity to light the table, candles are now used more for their decorative qualities. The choice is endless; different shapes, different colours, tall and slender, short and squat, plain and fancy, or even perfumed. Candles still cast a pleasant glow. Light a formal table with many elegant candles or reduce the number for a romantic atmosphere. Combined with flowers, greenery, driftwood or ribbon, candles make good table decorations or centre-pieces.

Candle shapes

Classic Venetian candles are the essence of dinner-table elegance. They are quite plain and smooth, tapering the entire length. Other traditional designs are straight-sided and have tapered butts to give a better grip and fit in the holder. These candles burn slowly and are well suited to large table-centre arrangements. Tall super-slim candles, often called 'flower lights', go well in the more delicate holders and massed in modern Scandinavian style flat candelabra. Together they give a gentle crown of light, decorative rather than brilliant. These candles are especially suited to fanned-out arrangements but are prettier arranged in one central display where guests are not expected to hand dishes among themselves. They are rather fragile! Sturdier arrangements, either in more traditional candelabra or single candle and flower combinations, are often safer.

Closely related to the classic taper come the spirals and twists. Very lovely when lit – they seem to have a quite distinctive flame – these are less formal, with a definite festive look. Red or white ones are ideal for use in a strong flower arrangement with vivid colours, such as a combination of Christmas holly, poinsettias and pine cones.

Totally different but equally lovely in their own way, are chunky candles of the pillar, ball or geometric shapes. Firm standing, and long burning, they make the liveliest of decorations. Dress them up with inflammable foil cut-outs and glass beads for a children's party; you can even give them funny faces.

In recent years a whole new world of candles in glass has been created. Little fairy lights, like night lights in their own coloured opaque holders burn for ten hours, so will outlast most parties. Wine glass and brandy balloon candles give a pleasing light without formality. Floating candles are a charming novelty. They feature a sherry-type glass with a wick and float, and a special liquid that burns with a red or green flame. Home-made floating candles are easy to contrive. You simply float a 'dock', fitted with a wick, on cooking oil in a wine glass. You can also buy coloured wax granules and wicks which enable you to make up all kinds of attractive effects in glass of your choice. This is a good idea if you pick up some unusual antique glasses in small numbers.

Candle holders and candelabra

Candle holders date from the earliest recorded times. Once, they were made from bronze, silver, gold, pewter and brass. Now you can choose from china, pottery, stoneware, glass, wood, as well as metal – the list is as endless as the different shapes. The newest idea in glass is the set of two or three matched glass sticks of differing lengths; this permits very beautiful asymmetrical effects.

Single candle holders are usually called sticks, and multiple candle holders, candelabra. Most people associate candelabra with a mighty, many-branched edifice, but there are more modest designs. Some, less than 12cm/4¾in high, are suitable for the dining-table, but others really only look well on a sideboard. Slender candles need a defined hole into which they can be placed. Many modern candle holders, however, are flat surfaced and fitted with a spike on to which the candles are pressed. You must be sure your candles are securely positioned to avoid accidents, even if this means twisting paper round the butt, so that it fits well into the stick. Wide-based, round, square or squat candles stand happily in a shallow saucer-like holder without support. If the holder does not please you it is often easy to hide it with flowers, greenery, or gilded pine cones.

Candle holders are easily improvized. Straw-covered chianti bottles and shaped rosé bottles are popular examples. Flowerpin holders, spiked steel meat platters, sand, shells, a piece of driftwood are other practical ideas. Moulded plasticine helps to make the candle stand up straight. Some containers, like egg-cups, might look secure but become top-heavy with the candle in position, so choose contrived holders that are reasonably sturdy.

Candle and flower arrangements
Candles and flowers look well together. There are no rigid rules, but the general principles of symmetry associated with flower arranging apply. Arm yourself with the same sort of materials – pin holders, plasticine, oasis, etc. Here are a few suggestions.

A large round posy ring (or four quarter-sized containers which together make a circle) provides an ideal basis. Space out the candles round the ring, anchoring them firmly in plasticine, and fill in between with short-stemmed flower heads and greenery. Instead of flowers you can use fir cones or large pasta shapes sprayed with gold or silver paint if you wish. The general effect can be varied to suit the occasion, for example for Christmas separate candles with fir tree cuttings, holly and miniature glass baubles. For weddings and christenings use white or coloured paper ribbon bows and flowers. It is now possible to obtain non-drip candles especially designed to be used with flower arrangements.

Tall single candle arrangements

Study the effect for balance as it may be better to have a tall single candle rising from a shallow stick, or a shorter candle rising from a fairly tall one. A stem of miniature ivy can be anchored in the stick as you position the candle, twined round the candle and fixed near the top with a short pin.

Trailers

To give an elaborate effect to the table without obscuring anyone's view, trailing flower and fern decorations can be led out towards the corners of the table from a central candle. A few blooms can be arranged round the candle base to give the centre-piece more importance. Dried flowers and seed heads are often better than fresh flowers for this sort of arrangement, because they will not droop when deprived of water. A candle 'cup', which you can buy from a florist, transforms a wine bottle into a holder, ideal for small flower heads, greenery or even bunches of grapes and trails of smilax or ivy.

Candle safety

Do ensure that holders are able to support the weight of the candle and that the arrangement is not top-heavy and liable to fall. Make sure that you do not put candles on to a table that is wobbly, or likely to be jogged in a crowded room. Candles in containers are safer when they are to be left alight in an empty room. An accident with lighted candles could easily spoil your party, so take extra care. If you stand candles on a buffet table against a window or wall, see that they are well clear of any curtains and the wall itself. A safe and economical decoration, suitable for teenage parties, can be made by covering jam jars with coloured crêpe paper, secured with an elastic band around the neck, and lowering a lighted nightlight carefully into each one.

FLOWERS AND VASES

When we come to the section on colour schemes for table layouts you will see that flowers and flower decorations form a most important part of this art. Any décor can be entirely altered by using flowers of a different colour arranged in different ways. So even if you have a limited supply of linens and china, you can still create many different effects with the use of flowers, especially imaginative designs requiring very few blooms.

Basic flower arranging

You will need quite a few basic materials as well as vases and bowls. Although impromptu bunches stay more or less in position, a proper arrangement may collapse unless it is firmly fixed in place. For this you need blocks of oasis, pin holders and crumpled chicken wire. A more professional effect is obtained if every flower stalk is individually wired. The wires come in various thicknesses according to the delicacy of the flower stem and for short stems a single wire can be cut in half with sharp scissors. The wire is pushed in near the flower head and bound to the stem with narrow, green florists' tape, which is stretchy and almost self-adhesive. One great advantage of taking this trouble is that you can move flower heads or wired trails of leaves fractionally after completing the arrangement without breaking delicate stems. This is more help than it sounds, since often your success or failure depends on being able to twist 'difficult' flower heads into exactly the right position. All these accessories can be bought at your florist.

Before you begin, decide on the container and its position. If it is to be in the centre of a table you would want a much lower arrangement than on a sideboard (not more than 20cm/8in high). Now decide on the basic shape. These follow certain forms, such as an oval, a diamond, a triangle or an 'S' curve. If you use large blooms you may decide on an oval or a triangle unless the blooms are tall and slender, in which case they will be better arranged in a flowing, almost horizontal shape rather than vertically. The choice of colour can influence the final result. A feeling of gentle harmony can be achieved by using two or more colours which are close to each other on the spectrum (the range of colours you see in the rainbow). Buy a colour wheel from a local art shop to help you in selecting colours. Another satisfying effect is made by using various tones of just one colour. A dramatic arrangement is best achieved by featuring contrasts. For example, yellow daffodils and purple irises in a spring arrangement.

Basic flower arrangement shapes

To begin work, take the flowers which are to be the main points of interest in your design and make sure that these will appear to all spring from a single point of origin, using foliage or short flower heads to conceal the stems. Now take other flowers, cut their stems to varying length and fill in the design radiating outwards from the focal point. No stems should be seen to cross others and make sure the foliage you use as a background covers them well. If you wish the arrangement to have a

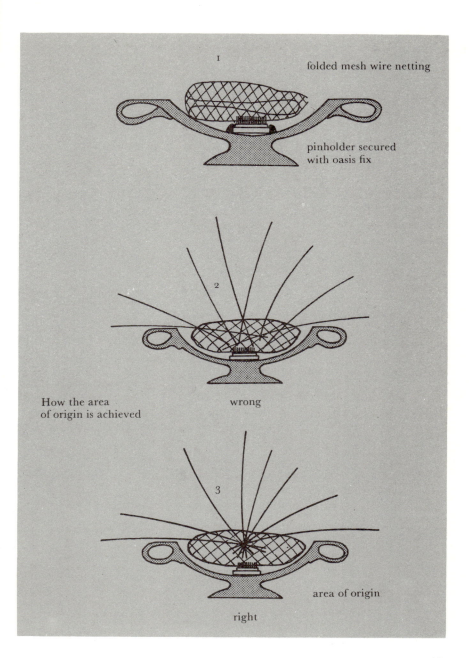

1

folded mesh wire netting

pinholder secured
with oasis fix

2

How the area
of origin is achieved

wrong

3

area of origin

right

45

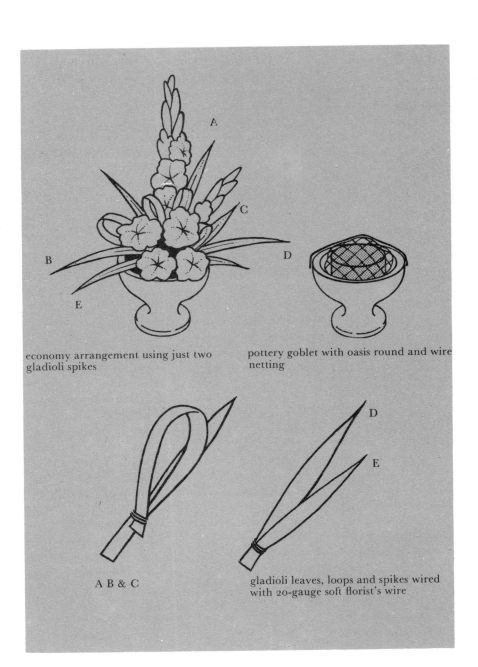

economy arrangement using just two gladioli spikes

pottery goblet with oasis round and wire netting

A B & C

gladioli leaves, loops and spikes wired with 20-gauge soft florist's wire

rather solid appearance, keep darker, stronger shades to the base and and lighter shades to the top of the arrangement. Dark colours appear to give weight, even though the flowers themselves may be delicate and light, and the visual balance is all-important. Since the lines in nature are not absolutely straight, aim at producing graceful curving effects. Remember that the container is also part of the balance and that the finished arrangement should not appear to be top-heavy. In any case, the container should not be so obtrusive that it distracts the eye from the arrangement itself.

Stand well back and appraise the finished arrangement; just one bloom may need to be repositioned, or there may be one empty patch to be filled.

Containers for flower arrangements

There is a wide selection of low, shallow containers available in the shops today made specially for table arrangements, but raid your kitchen or search the junk shops for suitable unusual containers. For example, fluted flan dishes, pie dishes, soup plates, soup bowls, jelly moulds, sauce boats and soufflé dishes, large wine glasses, old milk jugs and vegetable dishes will all provide interesting shapes.

Keep useful small jars and tins in which you can make a basic arrangement and which can be placed in an unusual holder. Since cracked or slightly damaged antiques can be bought cheaply, this overcomes the problem of water leaking from them. If the holder is too flat to conceal an actual container for the flowers, line it with polythene before filling with a damp oasis to make your arrangement.

How to treat fresh bought flowers

When buying flowers, make your choice according to the purpose for which they are required. Flowers suitable for a dinner party table arrangement are not necessarily those you would choose for their long-lasting qualities. Sometimes, fully developed flowers are sold more cheaply and are ideal for just one evening. Different flowers have different expectations of life. On the whole, autumn and winter flowers last longer when cut than spring and summer ones. Chrysanthemums are particularly hardy and are now available for a large part of the year.

Flowers naturally prefer cool, airy rooms but humidity is important to them too. In centrally-heated homes, the green foliage of house plants acts as a humidifier. Of course, all cut flowers need plenty of clean, cool water. If they wilt prematurely, they have probably either been deprived of water or the cut stem is 'sealed'. Using a slanting cut, snip the end of all stems before putting in water and hammer the ends of woody stems so that they can better absorb water. Always remove leaves which will be left below the water-level in the vase because they are bound to rot and pollute the water. If the florist advises shock treatment, stand the ends of long-stemmed flowers in a small amount of almost boiling water for a few minutes before plunging them into deep cold water. This sometimes revives roses that are drooping at the neck, just below the flower head.

Bought flowers should not be left lying around in their paper wrapping. As soon as you get them home, remove the wrapping and stand them in a bucket of water until you have time to arrange them. Other sources of trouble may be caused by putting your flowers in a draught or too close to a hot radiator. Finally, some flowers are heavy drinkers and unless you top up their containers daily they will dehydrate and droop before you change the water in the vase completely.

How to treat fresh garden flowers

As soon as possible after being picked, all flowers should be plunged into a deep bucket filled with lukewarm water and left there for a couple of hours to have a long cool drink.

Floppy flowers such as tulips, and sometimes roses, which bend their stems near the calyx, should be placed in a bucket with a thick newspaper wrapped tightly around them. This will straighten the stems and make arranging easier.

Woody-stemmed plants, such as rhododendrons, forsythia, roses and chrysanthemums, should have the ends lightly crushed with a hammer. This enlarges the area through which a bloom can absorb water.

Blooms with fleshy stems, such as stocks and snapdragons, are better plunged in moderately hot water after shortening the stem by $1 cm(\frac{1}{2}in)$ with a slanted cut.

All flowers benefit from having this slanted cut rather than a straight cut to enlarge the area which absorbs water.

Making the most of a few flowers

If a small number of flowers are to be used as a table centre there are several methods to try.

1 Snap off the flower heads and using some of the leaves from the stems, float the flowers with the leaves fanning out from underneath each flower head. This can be done in a shallow flower bowl or china

bowl similar to a bulb bowl.

2 Use the same principle again but supplement the flowers with floating shallow candles.

3 Fix a house plant with trailing foliage firmly in the centre of a bowl deep enough to conceal the pot. Pack oasis or crumpled chicken wire round the pot and fill with the flowers at your disposal, bringing out trailers from the plant between the flower heads.

Full-blown flower heads

1 Place a full-blown rose in a finger bowl at each place setting.

2 Place a bun tin, preferably one of the gold-finished non-stick variety, in the centre of the table. Place a full-blown flower head in each indentation with a few leaves to form a 'cushion'.

Flowers with fruit and vegetables

1 Arrange flowers with fresh or dried artichoke heads on a flat platter.

2 Arrange avocado pears with flowers on a wooden board.

3 Place bunches of black or green grapes alternately with large flower heads on a wreath of fresh green laurel leaves.

Drying garden flowers

Flowers suitable for drying are: Statice limonium, honesty, Chinese lanterns, cornflowers and helichrysum. The most common way to dry flowers is by air drying. Pick flowers when dry. Tie bunches with soft string, allowing room for the flowers heads so that they do not get crushed and dry distorted. Hang with the heads downwards in a cool, light, airy room until completely dry.

Some dried flower arrangements

1 As a formal centre-piece, a white bowl filled with fresh roses and fronds of dried gypsophilia.

2 If the table is crowded, a china or glass cakestand, with heads of helichrysum in all colours, pressed in to a dome of oasis.

3 For a formal arrangement when fresh flowers are unobtainable, dried flowers, seedheads and leaves arranged in a triangular format springing from a shallow bowl, using crumpled chicken wire.

PLACE CARDS AND MENUS

Place cards are useful when seating more than six people. It is amazing how people seem to mill around a table waiting for guidance where to sit, and even for a small dinner, it might be worth writing place cards. Although it is usual to seat men and women alternately, without placing wife by husband if possible, the important thing is to encourage a successful balance of lively and quiet personalities. Use a thin, firm card, fold in half lightly across the centre, and write each name on the lower half of a folded card. Describe your guest as 'Mrs J.A. Smith', 'Joan Smith' or 'Joan' depending on the degree of formality needed for the occasion. Put the cards towards the centre of the table close enough to the place setting to leave no doubt. Use white card, or tone with the table setting theme if preferred. For special occasions, or children's parties, the card can be decorated with drawings or tiny flowers fixed with a spot of adhesive. Children will like place cards cut into shapes.

For a really large party with more than one table, a seating plan might be needed. Draw the table plan like a ground plan, and print in the names of the guests so that when it is displayed they will be easy to read. Put it somewhere prominent and ask guests to check their seat places some time before the meal begins.

Menus are really fun to write, and it flatters your guests that you should take the trouble to write one if the meal is sufficiently important. It can be a plain card leaning against a glass, folded Christmas-card fashion, or folded horizontally like a place card. Write the word 'Menu' at the top, then the description of the meal (Luncheon or Dinner for instance) underneath. Under this write the date, centred. Centre the recipe titles for the successive courses, one under the other, ending if appropriate with coffee and liqueurs. Leave a space and write the names of the wines, in the order served, towards the bottom. Or omit the wines and finish with a decorative hand-drawn flourish.

The ingredients alone do not make the finished dish. It is the way you combine them and present the result that entitles you to be called a superb cook. The same applies to table layout and the presentation of food. So the placing and lighting of your table is important. The harmony of table surface or linen, glass, candles and flowers is equally important. Perhaps most important of all is the *setting* these create for the food and drink you offer at the meal. If the general effect is successful, you have mastered the art of tablecraft as well as that of cookery.

Part 2
How to design colour schemes and table presentations

Successful tablecraft is not merely a matter of choosing and assembling a co-ordinated table-setting trousseau. Much planning and forethought goes into the art of creating an elegant and appropriate décor for every meal and occasion. The more experience you have, the more versatile you will become in using your own table accessories in different ways – from simple settings for daily meals, to elaborate themes for grand occasions. Here is an ideal medium in which to express your own personal taste, just as you do in choosing your wardrobe of clothes. Fortunately, the rigid rules of etiquette in table setting have become more flexible, just as they have in the choice of dress. The one rule still valid today is that cutlery is laid in such a way that guests can judge which pieces to use for which course. If your table plan leaves no space for all the cutlery required, additional pieces can be brought in with individual servings of any course on the menu.

COLOUR SCHEMES

A table layout which pleases the eye must fit happily into its surroundings and therefore your style of furnishing governs your colour schemes to a great extent. If your dining room is panelled in golden pine with carpet and curtains in autumn tints, it would be wrong to choose a gay red-and-white gingham cloth for breakfast, no matter how attractive this may look in a different setting. Nor would this look particularly well with reproduction Regency furniture. Yet, brown-and-white gingham could set the mood for the meal and still remain on good terms with the dining room furniture.

CREATING A HARMONIOUS TABLE SETTING

The choice between buying patterned and plain china is often a difficult decision. It is easy to be charmed by one particularly beautiful design or a really unusual colour. In either case you might be restricting your ability to ring the changes on your table settings in the years to come. It is not always necessary to choose between a pretty pattern and plain china of elegant shape. An excellent solution is to build up a service of good, expensive china for entertaining and a second service in pottery for everyday use. You will find greater flexibility in table layout if one set is plain and the other patterned. When the china in daily use, as well as your best service, is patterned, you may find yourself investing in a second 'wardrobe' of table linens and mats to suit the second pattern, or concentrating on white and a few basic plain colours to suit both services. For those who have experienced this problem, yet find plain self-coloured china too stark, there is a happy medium: an embossed design within the china itself or a simple coloured rim or border which adds interest without introducing a bold pattern.

Here are some up-to-date ideas to help you create harmonious effects with patterned china.

1 Strongly-patterned china looks best set on a plain cloth which matches one of the colours in the pattern, or repeats the colour in a lighter or darker shade. It need not be the predominant colour. For instance, if there is a delicate pin-point yellow centre to flowers in the pattern, the china would look well on a toning yellow cloth.

2 Patterned china featuring only two colours, such as an all-over pattern of blue on white, can be set on a patterned cloth of the same two colours but preferably a geometric pattern if the china has a flower pattern. The napkins could be plain blue or white. Fashion favours the 'layered look' – yet another pattern in the same two colours for the napkins. This is only successful if the tablecloth is covered diagonally with a smaller one in the plain colour.

3 The two-colour scheme can be achieved in a different way. For instance, a coarse white lace tablecloth laid over a blue cloth which shows through the lace as a background for blue-and-white china. The theme should extend to the centrepiece which might in this case be created with white or blue candles and white flowers.

4 Another way to make a feature of strongly-patterned china is to place it on a white cloth with embroidered motifs taken from the china, or a wide braid border featuring the range of colours in the pattern. Napkins could be plain or matched to any one of the colours in the border.

5 For a festive table setting, choose white or off-white (if the background shade of your patterned china is cream rather than brilliant white) for the cloth. Pick out one colour from the bold pattern and use this for the napkins and for lengths of wide satin ribbon arranged across and down the centre of the table, interwoven like a basket in the centre. No other centre-piece is necessary.

If you want to put plain china in a pretty setting, try any one of these five ways.

1 Lay the china on a plain cloth which gives a stunning colour contrast.

For example, white china on a navy-blue or bottle green cloth; or dark brown pottery on an oatmeal or flame-coloured cloth. Search around for washable materials which blend together the two colours and tones to make pretty napkins; or keep to one of the two basic colours in the scheme.

2 Reveal your table-top and use patterned place-mats under the china. These may be heat-proof themselves, or made of material and laid over heat-proof mats. Patterned place-mats made of material often have colour-coded napkins. If you buy these in a set, make sure that spare napkins are available in the same colour as, for example, an extra one looks well used to line a basket for bread, or as a tray cloth for your coffee set.

3 Another version of the 'layered look' is to place a small patterned cloth over a plain cloth as a background for plain china. Napkins to go with this might be patterned or plain, or of a colour to pick up one of the tones in the pattern.

4 White china is, of course, the most versatile of all, and there are table-cloths or place mats in strong colours scalloped with white embroidery to match to go on a polished table surface. This gives a wonderfully clean, fresh-looking contrast.

5 One of the most popular of all plain pottery designs comes in definite pastel tones of blue, green and yellow. Match the pastel tone with a cloth and cover this with a white or écru (coarse) lace cloth. The colour of the china will be echoed by the cloth peeping through the lace. White or écru napkins to match the lace cloth will marry up the two-tone setting.

Simple and ornate cutlery and glass

The rules were once simple and easy to follow – silver cutlery and cut glass with fine china; stainless steel and chunky glassware with pottery. This rule no longer applies since shapes and designs in pottery are often as beautifully elegant as those in fine bone china. Many cutlery designs are available both in silver and stainless steel. While hand-made crystal is often deeply etched or engraved, machine-made glass is as beautiful in its own way because of its shape and sometimes because of its frosty-looking exterior finish. How then can you decide what cutlery and glass is compatible with your china and linen? Here are some suggestions on how to form your judgment.

1 Appraise visually whether the colour-scheme as a whole is subtle or bold. Decide whether the china and linen give a delicate or sub-

stantial effect. In the former case, plan to use cutlery and glass which fit in with a subtle and delicate layout. Decoration on the pieces should be, if ornate, not overpowering. Alternatively, use pieces that have little ornament but fine and graceful shapes. On the other hand, if the effect of china and linen is bold and substantial, chunky glass and heavier cutlery (possibly without any ornament) would blend in very well. The secret of such a successful arrangement is 'balance' of all the table accessories.

2 The choice of cutlery includes handles made of wood and different-coloured materials such as bone and stoneware. If a generally sparkling effect is preferred, light is brilliantly reflected from well-polished silver and cut glass. Silver goblets may deprive you of the sparkle of wine, but they do reflect light beautifully. Equally lovely is a table laid with bronze cutlery and goblets, which impart a golden glow to the whole setting. Solid pewter or satin-finished stainless steel with plain glass give a pleasant sheen. Condiment sets should match either the china or the metal. You may even prefer wooden-handled cutlery and matching teak condiment sets and salad bowls, to give a completely matt effect.

Completing the décor with candles and flowers

The balance of a table setting can be greatly influenced by the finishing touches. These include flower and candle arrangements and other items such as individual place cards, 'favours' or small presents wrapped to match the general colour scheme.

Here are three ways to complete the arrangement of a large table which appears to be rather sparsely set.

1 Make a large central arrangement of flowers in a low cushion shape with leafy trailers brought out towards each place setting. Arrange groups of tall slender candles either side. Variegated ivy is ideal for this purpose and after the party the cut ends will soon make roots if placed in water.

2 Instead of having a central candlestick or group of candles, place matching candlesticks or candelabra equidistant from the centre of an oblong or oval table. Fill in the empty space between them with a shallow tray or basket filled with fruit and exotic vegetables, if possible including a few gourds. Red and green peppers and aubergines, if polished, are extremely attractive in shape and colour. Be sure that the colour of the candles complements the colour of one of the fruits or vegetables.

3 To improvize a big space filler very quickly, arrange a group of chunky candles of differing heights and toning colours close together on a small tray, or teak platter, the tallest in the centre. The arrangement should not be completely symmetrical. If you do not have enough candles to make a good display, they could be grouped round an unusual wine bottle.

If your table is small and the setting crowded, try these decorative ideas instead.

1 Place a single, tall, candlestick in the centre of the table. It must be quite a sturdy and impressive one to have the right eye-catching effect. To dress this up even more effectively, twist a trail of ivy or tinsel ribbon around the candle.

2 Fold the napkins in a mitre shape and place in the glasses, leaving the side plates free for rolls and pats of butter if there is no room to place a bread basket or butter dish on the table.

3 Make a decorative feature of the napkins by rolling them, fixing with a ring of self-adhesive gift ribbon and passing a tiny spray of flowers through the ring. Place on the side plates.

4 Make a centre-piece like a crown of tall slender candles, rising in a circle from a small saucer-shaped holder. If liked, fill in the base with small bunches of grapes, or a mixture of nuts in the shell and large pasta shapes sprayed with paint. The grapes of course can form part of the menu but the nuts will be strictly ornamental!

The height of glasses, flower arrangements and candles is important. Tall slender candles look better with long-stemmed fine glasses than with squat chunky ones. Since a flower arrangement can be varied according to your own taste, decide on the wine glasses and candles first and use the placing of the flowers to create a harmonious effect.

TABLE-SETTING TECHNIQUES

When you set the table, you also set the mood for the meal. Much more goes into it than extracting so many plates, knives and forks from cupboards and drawers. For any meal to be truly successful, everything in the room you use for eating must combine to set the mood you want; the lights, the furniture, the table linen too. An atmosphere of comfort, warmth, (or coolness on a blazing hot day) relaxation and expectation of enjoyment should be aimed at. Here is how to do it.

Single Place Settings

informal lunch

family meal

modern-style family lunch

family celebration dinner

5 course dinner for guests

4 course dinner for guests

The golden rules of table setting

Decide which accessories you propose to use. Sometimes a cloth that has been badly folded requires a touch of the iron; so do napkins, using a little spray starch, before folding. You may have alternative choices of coloured candles, and these need bringing out of store. There may be flowers to be picked at the last minute in the garden, or some fresh greenery from your hedge. For everyday meals it may be all perfectly simple, but for entertaining, take no chances. Unless your memory is extra keen, make a note of all you will need.

Lay the table with cloth or mats first, holding washable-surfaced mats to the light to make sure they have not got any lingering traces of a previous meal. Polish if need be. Set the cutlery next, polishing with a soft, dry, cloth as you handle each piece. Now come the glasses, and again a little dry polishing may be needed to bring up the shine. Count out the pieces of china you will need, and lay the table ready for the first course, making sure salt and pepper shakers are filled. Now you can see how much space you have for extra condiment sets, bread baskets, butter dishes, and the other small paraphernalia of table setting, to be balanced by some decorative effect. Traditional candles and a centre-piece of polished fruit? A low flower arrangement with delicate slim candles springing from it? Sometimes the decoration lightens a rather ponderous table setting. Try to bring about a balance; remembering that decorative touches should be lighter in feeling, fresher, and more delicate in their harmony than the implements of eating but if too fragile in effect, the contrast might be too great and it may draw attention to the heaviness of solid stoneware or pistol-handled cutlery.

Complete these last touches and walk round the table to make sure it looks as good from every place setting as from your own chair. If candles might drip, guard against this by putting them in the freezer for the time you take to cook the meal. Renew any that are burned more than halfway down from the top; no table looks pretty illuminated with guttering candle ends. Make use of reflection. If there is a mirror any-where in the dining room it should reflect the table setting or a flower piece on the sideboard in a flattering manner, and not, for instance, the door into the kitchen.

Formal meal settings

For a meal with several courses, forks are all laid on the left of the place settings, knives and spoons on the right, working from the outside inwards as the pieces are required. The rounded side of a knife blade is always laid inwards. If there are *more* than two courses laid before the sweet, it is quite usual to set the dessert spoon and fork horizontally outside the place setting. This would be the case if, for example, the first course required a soup spoon, then there was a fish course, followed by meat or poultry. So in the most formal type of setting you would find a small bread knife or hors d'oeuvre knife outside on the right, then a soup spoon (if served), with a fish knife inside, a large knife for meat or poultry inside this; and last of all, on the inside a dessert spoon. On the left would be a small fork for hors d'oeuvre (if served) then a fish fork, a larger fork inside this for meat or poultry and finally a dessert fork. Four-course meals are rare today, but the dessert setting may still be kept separate from the earlier courses.

An imposing array of cutlery on the table sometimes detracts from its charm. You can avoid the 'serried ranks' by placing the bread knife on the side plate, at an angle or straight, or on a folded napkin. The cutlery needed for the first course, if it is an hors d'oeuvre rather than a soup, may be laid on the plate ready for eating. This course is placed on top of the plate which will be used for the second course; a grapefruit spoon on a small plate next to the grapefruit half in a sundae dish or footed dessert dish; or a small fork next to a prawn cocktail in a wine-glass on a small plate. The same method works well if the first course is melon, or any sort of exotic fruit or shellfish cocktail.

Other items of cutlery are usually served with the course, as required, to avoid having too many pieces laid at the start of the meal. If dessert fruit is offered, special cutlery with pearl or fancy handles may be passed round with the plates.

If there is no course between the hors d'oeuvre and the main one, the largest instead of the medium-sized plate should be set under it – unless you intend to bring in the main course ready served out, or to set hot plates for it. Some people find a whole dinner is spoiled for them if they are offered hot food on cold plates.

Serving from table or sideboard
When tables were large, and joints of meat enormous, it was quite usual for the host to carve and serve out portions for all on to a pile of hot plates in front of him, while the hostess served vegetables and sauces at the other end of the table. This presupposed a servant to carry plates to and fro, something we hardly expect to see now outside a hotel or restaurant. It is quite normal for the main course to be dealt with as follows.

1 The hostess places covered vegetable dishes, sauce boats and salad bowls on the table, and the main dish in front of the host. He carves or serves out, and hands the filled plates to guests, who help themselves from the vegetable dishes, passing them round from one to the other. This has the disadvantage that by the time all have been served, some guests are often politely waiting for the ritual to be complete with a plate of food cooling in front of them.

2 The hostess swiftly serves all the accompaniments from a hot plate on the table or sideboard and distributes the filled plates herself before sitting down again. Covered dishes and sauce boats remain on a heated stand, preferably an electric hotplate, on the sideboard or a trolley, to keep the food hot for second helpings. If the meal is a complicated one to serve, you may prefer to avoid long drawn-out urgings and coy refusals of second helpings, and merely remove the plates when the last guest has finished the course.

3 The whole meal can be served out in the kitchen and packed into an electrically-heated hostess trolley, which is then wheeled into place close enough to the hostess to enable her to serve everyone including herself quickly.

4 It is usual to place the salad bowl and dressing on the table at the same time as the main course as some people like to eat salad with the hot food while others like to serve it out on a separate side plate. Have small plates ready to replace those used for salad, as bread and butter plates for the cheese course. If you are short of such small plates, put small glass salad dishes or teak bowls outside the place settings on the left to balance the glasses on the right.

Table for two

Usually this is a small round table or occasional square table – probably a card table. Set the two places facing, and then you will see what space you have for decorative touches. At night, indoors, candles are close enough to cast a romantic glow on both diners. If eating on a balcony or terrace, a candle in a storm lantern, or protected by glass would be ideal. When cooking for two, it is easier for the hostess to make the meal enjoyable if everything is fully prepared before sitting down, or waiting may be agonizing for one impatient guest who has no-one to talk to while you disappear for minutes on end. A cold first course ready set on the table gets the meal off to a good start, and the main course could be ready-served out on plates keeping warm under a low grill or in the oven.

Small tables out of doors

When the alternative is to hire trestle tables and benches, you may prefer to bring into service all the small tables you have, including those which are normally kept in the garden. They can be given an air of teamwork by covering them all with matching cloths. Even on a day with little wind, cloths tend to blow about, but café clips can be used to hold them firmly on the table at the edges. If you do not have many matching cloths, make a rainbow assortment, and cover them all with small, matching, disposable paper cloths, of an eye-catching colour, and place tumblers of fanned out paper napkins in the same colour on each table. This is quite sufficient to team up a motley assortment of tables. The same applies to china, which may not match. The use of a few paper serving plates or tumblers on all the tables in the same gay colour as the cloth will provide a useful link.

Setting a tea-table

This is rather different from the conventional place setting of other formal meals, as the individual settings only consist of a small plate, folded napkin, and cake fork or small knife if creamy gâteaux or hot buttered teacakes which need cutting are on the menu. The cups and saucers, complete with teaspoons, are ranged in front of the hostess, together with the milk jug, sugar basin and teapot. Hot water in a thermos jug is a useful stand-by. Otherwise, rinse out a lidded jug (perhaps one used for coffee) with boiling water, then fill with freshly boiled water to hold the heat. This, and the teapot, should stand on a heat-proof mat. The savoury items such as sandwiches, scones, and bread and butter should be ranged round the outer part of the table, for guests to help themselves. Jam or honey should be served out in glass dishes with spoons, not left in the pots. In the centre of the table, place fancy cakes, biscuits and gâteaux, as the savoury items will be eaten first. It looks more attractive if all the serving plates are covered with matching paper doileys before arranging the contents.

When tea is served informally, and not seated at table, the hostess should have a low table or trolley close to her, holding the tea things, cups and saucers, and she should hand each guest a cup of tea, placing the saucer on a tea plate with a folded napkin, then serving plates of food. See to it that guests, whether sitting in armchairs or on the sofa, have a low table nearby for their own cups and saucers, napkins and plates. The food must be handed round, so it is better to avoid messy foods, which require cutting or forks. Most helpful is a three-tier cake stand on which items can be displayed for which there will be no room on the trolley. This allows guests to see what there is since many will choose to eat only one or two sandwiches if there is a favourite cake still to come. However careful you are, there will probably be crumbs if not jammy smears on the carpet afterwards, so be prepared.

Setting a coffee table

This almost indispensable piece of furniture now serves a far wider range of purposes. Almost any snack meal can be served from the coffee table. If the surface is not heat-proof, any hot plates of food, and the coffee pot, should all be placed together on a heat-proof tray or large mat. The individual plates can be stacked, using napkins as separaters, and handed out together with the cutlery that is needed. But as with informal tea, the service goes more smoothly if the menu is limited to easily negotiated finger foods; guests will be embarrassed if food or drink is spilled on the carpet. A small nest of three occasional tables, if strategically placed, will serve the needs of all the guests who who cannot find room on the coffee table even to put down a cup.

Setting a sideboard

For parties where a substantial buffet meal is part of the programme, most sideboards are too small to hold all the food. When the occasion is a christening, or the celebration of a wedding anniversary, the important event is the cutting of a decorated cake, accompanied by a special toast, drunk if possible in champagne. Other sparkling white wines are equally suitable, possibly a French wine in the Veuve du Vernay category, or a German Sekt. As these affairs tend to be less formal, with fewer guests than at a wedding, the sideboard can be used rather than covered trestle tables.

The sideboard setting is similar to that of a buffet table, with the distinct limitation that it can only be approached from one side. This is the ideal occasion to use tall flower pieces, rising well clear of the table top, difficult for an amateur to arrange for all-round viewing, but easy to achieve if only seen from the front and sides. Gaps at the back can always be filled in with foliage or less-than-perfect blooms. Remember that guests will probably all be approaching the sideboard at the same time, so spread out the food and accessories to avoid queuing.

Christening buffet

This can be far more colourful than a wedding buffet, which is usually more formal and follows an all-white theme. Concentrate on pink or blue, according to the baby's sex. Shades can range from delicate pastel to rich toning colours depending on the flowers in season. With very strong colours in the flower arrangements it might be wise to use white rather than coloured ribbon.

If you have a pretty patterned china with even a hint of pink or blue in it, use this. It will tone in with the flowers you choose to carry on the general theme. Place the christening cake centrally on the sideboard, slightly raised on a tray; after all, it is the focus of attention. Put tall flower arrangements at either end of the sideboard and if it is a long one, a lower toning arrangement on each side of the cake. Leave room for glasses and wine bottles on one side, tea or coffee with cups set ready on the other, next to small plates of finger foods. Guests can take a glass of wine, admire the cake, pass on and help themselves to a nibble or two. After the toast to the baby, the cake is cut, and it is usually whisked away to be quickly sliced up. Have a really sharp, even if inelegant, knife ready in the kitchen. While the cake is being handed round, guests will return more slowly for a hot drink and further selection from the dishes of food on the sideboard. Children can be served with cold fruit squash in paper cups from a tray on a side table. If handled in this way, the whole plan is rather like that for a cocktail party, as refreshments on these occasions are no longer expected to be of the substantial sit-down variety.

Buffet table set against the wall
Although not as limited in space as a sideboard setting party, the guests at a buffet party are likely to be more numerous, and the choice of food much wider if the buffet is to provide a whole meal. Simply placing your dining table (fully extended) along one wall and removing the chairs often provides plenty of room for guests to approach the table comfortably. Work out a simple plan and prevent awkward collisions by arranging items in the order they will be collected. If possible, repeat the arrangement starting at both ends and meeting in the middle, so guests can serve themselves more easily. The decorative arrangements should stand at the back of the table, and may be symmetrical (matching flower and candle groups at each end) or asymmetrical (tall flower arrangement one end, and piled-up fruit bowl on a stand at the other). If there is one hot dish, say boeuf stroganoff and rice, this may have to be placed at one end on a plate warmer with a pile of plates to keep hot. A partially carved turkey, ham, or joint of beef, to provide a substantial

cold alternative, could go at the other end. In front of these main dishes, pile medium-sized plates, napkins and cutlery. Between the two ends, place bowls of salad, sauce boats of mayonnaise and French dressing, baskets of cut bread, rolls or crispbreads and dishes of butter. In the centre (to which guests will return later) a selection of desserts – sliced gâteaux, trifles, fruit salads, jugs of cream – and in front of these, smaller plates and the necessary cutlery.

It is really more satisfactory to dispense drinks from a separate trolley, or the sideboard, or even a covered card table. Any convenient window ledge or mantelpiece should be provided with pretty paper glass mats, so that guests can put down their drinks somewhere. Try to limit the food to that which can be handled with a fork, and does not require a knife as well. No-one can hold a plate and wield both knife and fork at the same time. Glasses only need small perching places so these can be put down while holding the plate with one hand and the fork with the other. Desserts should also be of the kind which can be eaten with a cake fork or small spoon. Towards the end of the meal, clear one end of the buffet table of savoury dishes, and put everything you need for the service of coffee in their place. Always plan ahead for the disposal of used plates, as these look rather sordid if just carelessly laid down anywhere.

This arrangement presupposes that guests will stand about in the room where the buffet is served while they eat. If there is another room where they can sit at small tables, or outside on a terrace, there is no need to place cutlery and napkins on the buffet table. Napkins can be folded round a few pieces of cutlery, to provide each person with everything needed for the meal, and placed on the tables where they will sit. It is even possible to lay plates, with the folded napkins and cutlery on top. Each guest then takes a plate up to the buffet and fills it. If room for food is really cramped, this saves valuable space for extra dishes.

Buffet table set away from the wall

The arrangement of such a table is more complicated than the table against the wall, because it must look well from every angle. The decorative element has to be central, or at each end, well away from the edge. The table should be placed end on to the length of the room, so that people can flow easily round it, and have good access to the short sides. Candle sticks are liable to be knocked over; a good centre-piece would be a flower and fruit arrangement, or merly an arrangement of delectable fruit. A mixture of green and black grapes always looks well,

66

and small bunches can be broken off by guests. Frost some of them, preferably the green grapes, by brushing with lightly-beaten egg white and dipping in caster sugar.

Plates and cutlery can all be stacked in low piles at either end of the table. Begin with the main hot dish on the left at the near end of the table, and continue with salads, sauces, bread and sweets up to the far end. On the other side of the table, begin with the cold main dish on the right at the far end, and graduate down to the sweets at the near end. This will allow guests to approach the table from opposite ends at both sides, and prevent hold-ups in service. If the food is grouped so that all the starters are at one end and the sweets at the other, those who want their dessert will have to push past people still helping themselves to the first course. Try to persuade your guests to serve themselves a few at a time. There is no magic method of setting a table which will prevent polite pushing and shoving if twenty or more people suddenly try to serve themselves simultaneously.

Another idea to help service in a small space is to have duplicate dishes of those you know will soon be cleared, in the kitchen. As soon as popular dishes are empty, remove them and put in full dishes instead. This saves laying enormous platters of such favourites as potato and Russian salads.

TRAY ARRANGEMENTS

Breakfast tray: Spread with a clean tray cloth, lay with a place setting for one; small tea pot or coffee pot, milk jug and sugar and a small dish of butter pats or curls. Add letters or a folded newspaper. On the breakfast plate put a dish of cereal, or half a grapefruit in a glass dish, segmented with a curved grapefruit knife. It is difficult to present a breakfast tray with everything on it as hot as you could wish, so get it all ready with these items first. Next, make the tea or coffee. Then place a warm croissant or freshly made toast on a side plate, with a napkin to match the tray cloth and, if liked, a boiled egg in an egg-cup above centre of the first course. You will also need salt and pepper shakers. There is no way to provide hot crisp bacon and fried or scrambled eggs on the tray and keep them hot, unless by covering with a silver cover, or an inverted soup plate, but this does require a very large tray. If there is a tiny corner of space to spare, add a single bloom in a miniature vase.
Invalid tray: Since invalids have notoriously capricious appetites, the tray should be prepared with extra care. Spread a clean tray cloth, and

lay with a place setting for one, as for a normal meal. Fold the napkin on the side plate with a crisp warm roll inside it. Serve out the main course chosen with regard to contrast in colour, flavour and texture, cover immediately with a warmed inverted soup plate, and place the dessert in a small dish above left, a flower posy above centre, and a glass or water tumbler, perhaps filled with milk, above right. Garnish the main dish with parsley sprigs, then lemon slices, or whatever you choose to make the plate especially appetising when the cover is removed.

Television tray: Many people would rather eat a snack meal from a tray than miss a favourite programme. The setting is completely informal, but few want to be bothered with a cup and saucer. Hot soup or a hot drink in a mug would be appropriate. The main course, served on a dessert plate, could be sandwiches or a meat salad in a shallow bowl with a few savoury biscuits round the edge of the plate. If the tray has a clean tray cloth, the napkin might be tied in a loose single knot, or slipped into a napkin ring. No-one expects a three-course meal on a TV tray, and indeed the food should be as simple as possible. Add either a piece of fruit with a dessert knife on a side plate, or a flower posy, to fill the space.

TABLE DISPLAYS FOR BIG OCCASIONS

It is not usually necessary to call in professional caterers or florists to create a beautiful table setting. For a large number of guests you may have to hire trestle tables but these can be covered with lightly-starched white sheets to take the place of the enormous table-cloths of yesteryear. Even pale pastel sheets can be used to beautiful effect. China, cutlery and glassware can all be hired, or you can use disposable paper tableware with a decoration appropriate to the occasion. Borrowing sets of cutlery and china from friends not only involves work sorting it out afterwards, but sometimes a precious item, or just one teaspoon from a set of six, disappears, causing a rift between even the best of friends.

Wedding buffets

A wedding buffet looks best laid out on white table-cloths. (Or pastel blue, pink or yellow cloths if this tones in with the bridesmaids' dresses.)

Opposite A christening buffet can be more colourful than a wedding buffet. Concentrate on pink or blue, according to the baby's sex.

It is customary for the wedding cake to take pride of place in the centre of the table.

There are many ways in which the table itself can be decorated.

1 Swags can be used to decorate the front of the table. These are made of rolled florist's ribbon, looped and held to the edge of the table with drawing-pins. Bunches of roses (stems placed in damp cottonwool and wrapped in foil cones) are then pinned to the cloth to cover the drawing-pins. Fix garlands of more ribbon from the top of the cake to the back corners.

2 Make loops of different lengths using four strands of ribbon 2.5cm/1in wide, pinned to the edge of the table. Bunches of dried or paper flowers with a few silver leaves are then fixed to hide the drawing-pins. If you have a coloured cloth, use white ribbons and flowers.

3 Pin looped Smilax creeper to the edge of the table. Add bows of white or coloured ribbon with long trailing ends and fix to hide the pins. To make swags and garlands, attach bunches of Smilax to a thin rope or washing line with Sellotape – grading the thickness of the swags so that they are thickest at the base.

Using drawing pins or other methods of fastening decorations securely to the table, of course only applies to trestle tables concealed by cloths.

Left A buffet table always looks attractive with matching flower and candle groups. Plates are stacked in low piles for your guests to serve themselves.

71

2

3

If you are using a large dining table, decorations must be pinned to the cloth itself. To ensure that the weight of decorations does not pull the cloth forward on the table, fix the cloth at the back firmly by attaching it to a tape tied round the legs, or place weighty items at regular intervals along the back edge.

Silver or golden wedding buffets

It is quite easy to carry out a silver or golden theme with the table decorations.

Silver wedding Place glass or silver candlesticks at intervals down the back of the table, holding tall white candles. Surround the bases of the candlesticks with laurel leaves sprayed with silver paint and arrange in the shape of a wreath. Join the leaf sprays together with bunches of tiny silver baubles.

Golden wedding Arrange glass, bronze or brass candlesticks at intervals down the table, holding white or golden yellow candles. Surround bases with laurel leaves sprayed with gold paint joined together with sprays of bronze and yellow chrysanthemums and small golden baubles.

It it is a really big anniversary party, any of the 'Wedding' décor ideas could be carried out in colours echoing the silver or gold themes.

Decorating a cake table

Sometimes it is preferred to place a special cake for a wedding or 21st birthday on a table separate from the food. A small round or square table is ideal, covered with a cloth which hangs down to the floor. Shape and pin neat corner folds if it is a square table. Over the base cloth place a much smaller cloth, diagonally if for a square table. For a round table gather the smaller, round cloth up into ruched scallops and pin to the base cloth at the table edge. Cover the pins with small flower sprays. Place the cake either in the centre of the table, or slightly to one side with a flower arrangement behind it to make an asymmetric grouping.

Christmas party tables

Here are some simple and effective ways to decorate a Christmas table.
1 All that is required is a white table-cloth or sheet depending on the shape and the size of the table. Use florist's ribbon about 10cm/4in wide. Form a cross by sectioning your table into quarters, using two long strips of ribbon. Secure the centre by using pins or Sellotape so that it does not move around. On this centre join place a large double

bow. Attach the ends of the ribbon strips under the edge of the tablecloth in the centre of each side. The ribbon can be Christmas red or holly green and the bow takes the place of a table centre-piece. Baubles can be added to make the setting even more festive.

2 Spray a cheap wicker basket with gold paint. Fill it with apples and oranges, and walnuts also sprayed with gold paint. Pile them high up in the basket. Place on a white cloth in the centre of the table.

3 Make a wreath out of entwined ivy trails and arrange silver-sprayed pine cones at intervals. To keep the ivy trails in place, loosely bind them with red ribbon. Place in the centre of a polished table-top.

Children's parties

There are two ways to provide an exciting theme to set the table. If you prefer to use your own china, create novelty place mats, cutting them from coloured card or paper. Make a centre-piece which links small gifts for the children to place cards and insist that the children do not 'change places'. Confusion reigns when small guests dash about deciding who will sit next to whom!

Tableware that saves washing-up

Another way to please small guests is to use disposable tableware and table-cloths with a home-made centre-piece. If you are not offering the children individual gifts, place a small trifle or jelly by every plate. A simple table-setting for a children's tea-party is a 'bird of paradise' made from coloured paper tissues in the middle of the table. Place an exotic egg in the nest under the bird. After the meal you can announce that foil-covered chocolate eggs are hidden in various places in the room and allow the children to search for them. Be sure they are not so placed that snatching at them will cause any disaster such as knocking over small pieces of furniture.

Part 3
Meal presentation

You need not necessarily be an exceptionally skilled cook to present a delightful meal. The secret lies in planning the menu beforehand and co-ordinating it with the table setting. A purple-red Borscht soup might not look appetizing in sunshine yellow bowls whereas it would look glorious in white or pale green dishes. Although you might enjoy creamy mushroom soup, chicken fricassée and junket on separate occasions, as three courses of the same meal they would look insipid.

MENU PLANNING

Your aim should be two-fold: to create contrast of colour, texture and flavour in the food, without choosing colours which quarrel with your china or flower scheme. If in fact the basic colour of successive dishes is rather similar, you can alter the effect by using interesting garnishes. Cream of mushroom soup could be scattered with finely chopped parsley, and the chicken fricassée bordered with well-browned piped mashed potato and thin slices of lemon. Even the junket could provide another colour contrast if the surface were sprinkled with ground cinnamon or grated chocolate. Texture and flavour contrasts can be contrived with the choice of vegetables or salads to serve with the main dish. For the menu mentioned above, green peas would be better than Jerusalem artichokes, and a tomato salad or watercress and orange salad. With carrots as vegetables, a green salad would be ideal. To prevent the sameness of a creamy texture throughout, serve miniature brandy snaps with the junket, or an assorted fresh fruit salad.

Avoid serving three very rich dishes in succession. If your main dish is heavy, begin with a fruit or salad-type starter and finish with something like a light mousse or whole oranges in caramel sauce. If the main dish is less substantial, you could offer a velvety soup to begin with and a crème brulée for dessert.

MAKING A WORK PLAN

When you have to cook a meal for quite a few people, which involves more than two courses, you may find yourself wasting a great deal of time unless you make a work plan. Consider the desired end result first, which is that every course should be complete and ready to serve in the correct order. This may mean that you will prepare the cold dessert first of all and store it safely in the refrigerator while you prepare the rest of the meal. A hot pudding has to be prepared and be ready to go into the oven so that it will complete cooking after the earlier courses are served. It is a good general rule to decide what can be fully prepared beforehand and kept cold until needed (such as a trifle), or reheated at the last moment (such as a soup or an odorous curry). It is bad psychology to greet your guests with a pervading smell of curry which has been stealing through the whole house for the past two hours. Allow yourself sufficient time for activities connected with the meal which do not actually involve cooking – laying the table, folding napkins and arranging flowers. Put wine to chill if necessary and prepare fiddly items for garnishes and decorations while you have plenty of patience before the cooking is in full swing. Remember that blending in the liquidizer or beating with a rotary whisk are noisy activities and it is better to get these over with before guests arrive. Do not forget your own appearance and set aside somewhere in the work plan time to change and see to your make-up. Try to keep this as late in the day as possible so that you are not tempted to rush back into the kitchen in your party dress and carry out messy procedures like pouring gravy from a saucepan into a gravy boat. If you must, have an apron at the ready to protect your clothes from spots and splashes.

HOT BUFFET for 12 people

MENU

Kipper Pâté
Melon and Ginger Cocktails*

Seafood Vol-au-Vents
Boeuf Bourguignonne
Green Salad Courgettes
Potatoes au Gratin

Apricot Cheesecake
Fresh Pineapple with Kirsch
Cheeseboard
Sherry   Wine   Coffee

WORK PLAN

The Night Before
 1 Make Kipper Pâté and chill.
 2 Make Apricot Cheesecake and chill.

In the Morning
 3 Make up Melon and Ginger Cocktails and chill (they need at least 2 hours).
 4 Bake vol-au-vent cases. Make up seafood sauce, and keep covered.
 5 Slice fresh pineapple and marinate in Kirsch, covered.
 6 Prepare Courgettes.
 7 Make up Potatoes au Gratin ready for cooking.
 8 Prepare Salad ingredients.

2 Hours before Buffet
Lay the table . . . Prepare the wine . . . Grind the coffee
 9 Make up Boeuf Bourguignonne and put into oven to cook in a covered casserole. (180°C, 350°F, Gas Mark 4).

1 Hour before Buffet

10 Put Potatoes au Gratin into oven to cook.

30 minutes before Buffet

11 Cook courgettes and keep warm in oven on lower shelf.

12 Heat vol-au-vent cases through in oven. Heat sauce in double saucepan. Fill vol-au-vents and return to oven to keep warm.

13 Make up salad.

Just before buffet

14 Make toast for pâté.

* RECIPE

2 honeydew melons
6 pieces preserved stem ginger
1 tablespoon brandy
125ml/¼ pint fresh orange juice

Scoop the flesh from melons into small balls. Put into a bowl and add ginger, finely chopped. Mix brandy with orange juice. Spoon over melon balls and stir gently. Cover with cling wrap and chill.

DINNER PARTY for 6 people

MENU

Stilton and watercress pâté*
Beef olives

Duchess potato nests with peas
Glazed carrots

Caramelized oranges
Wine: Rosé
Coffee

WORK PLAN

In the Morning

1 Make up pâté and put into small pots. Chill, ready for serving.

2 Make up Caramelized Oranges and chill ready for serving.

3 Flatten meat for Beef Olives – spread with stuffing, roll up and tie.

4 Peel, cook and mash potatoes. Pipe into nests on baking sheet.

5 Peel and slice carrots.

90 minutes before Dinner

Lay the table . . . Prepare the wine . . . Grind the coffee

6 Finish preparing Beef Olives. Put into oven to cook in covered casserole (190°C, 375°F, Gas Mark 5).

30 minutes before Dinner

7 Cook carrots, and cook peas ready to fill potato nests. Keep warm, covered in oven.

8 Put potato nests in oven to brown.

Just before Dinner

9 Make toast for pâté.

* RECIPE

2 bunches watercress
250ml/½pint double cream
225g/½lb Stilton
1 garlic clove
Salt and pepper

Wash watercress and shake dry. Remove leaves and put into liquidizer with double cream, Stilton, garlic and seasoning. Blend until smooth. Pack into small cocotte dishes. Chill.

COLD BUFFET for 20 people

MENU

Chilled Cucumber Soup
Stuffed Eggs
Chilled Chicken Curry*
Spinach Quiche

Salmon Mousse
Potato and Walnut Salad
Mixed Salad
Rice Salad

Apple Flan   Summer Pudding
Cheeseboard
Chilled Wine Punch

WORK PLAN
The Night Before

1 Make up Salmon Mousse and chill.
2 Make Summer Pudding and weight overnight.
3 Make up pastry for flan and quiche; make up Apple Flan, minus glaze.
4 Cook chickens if you have bought uncooked ones.
5 Make up Chilled Cucumber Soup, and store covered in refrigerator.
6 Hard boil eggs for Stuffed Eggs.
7 Make up a bulk quantity of dressing for the salads.

In the Afternoon
Lay the table . . . Grind the coffee . . . Chill white wine

8 Make up Chilled Chicken Curry and put in the refrigerator.
9 Stuff hard boiled eggs.
10 Make up Spinach Quiche and cool.
11 Cook potatoes and make up Potato and Walnut Salad while they are still warm.
12 Cook rice and make up Rice Salad while it is still warm.
13 Glaze Apple Flan.

Just before Buffet
14 Make up Mixed Salad.
15 Make up wine punch using chilled wine.

*RECIPE
3 chickens, cooked
500ml/½ pint mayonnaise
500ml/½ pint soured cream
1 lemon
6 tablespoons curry powder
2 teaspoons salt
100g/4oz sultanas
salted peanuts to garnish

Skin cooked chickens and remove all the flesh in strips. Mix mayonnaise with soured cream, the grated rind and juice of lemon, curry powder, salt and sultanas. Stir in the chicken. Chill for at least 4 hours. Sprinkle with a few salted peanuts before serving.

OVEN-TO-TABLE DINNER for 6 people
MENU

Onion and Celery Soup
Chicken with Orange and Green Pepper Sauce
Baked Jacket Potatoes
Salad
Apple Streudel

WORK PLAN

1 Peel and slice 3 onions. Finely chop 4 stems celery. Fry vegetables gently in 3 tablespoons butter in large casserole. Add 2 stock cubes, 1 litre (approx. 2 pints) water, 1 tablespoon brown sugar, 1 tablespoon vinegar and seasoning. Cover and place in coolest part of oven.
2 Fry 6 chicken joints in 3 tablespoons butter until golden. Put chicken into large casserole. Fry 1

chopped onion in butter remaining in pan. Add 2 green peppers, cut into strips, and fry for a few few minutes. Add 250ml ($\frac{1}{2}$ pint) orange juice and 375ml ($\frac{3}{4}$ pint) milk, thickened with 2 tablespoons cornflour. Season. Pour sauce over chicken. Cover casserole and place on top shelf of oven.

3 Scrub 12 small potatoes and prick all over with a skewer. Place on top shelf, around casserole.

4 Peel, core and slice 750g (approx. 1$\frac{1}{2}$lb) cooking apples. Mix 175g (6oz) white breadcrumbs with 50g (2oz) demerara sugar and grated rind of 1 lemon and pinch ground nutmeg. Put half breadcrumb mixture into base of greased ovenproof dish. Pack in apple slices, adding an extra 50g (2oz) demerara sugar. Cover with remaining crumb mixture. Dot with 50g (2oz) butter. Place on middle shelf of oven.

5 Set oven to 180°C, 350°F, Gas Mark 4, to switch on 1 hour before meal is required.

Serving Instructions

Make croûtons to serve with soup. Make up salad and dressing. Split potatoes and fill with butter.

WINES AND OTHER DRINKS

First of all comes the aperitif. This is frequently a sherry or vermouth which you offer your guests as they arrive. It is much better to offer a simple choice than to say 'What would you like to drink?', as this gives them no guideline. Dry sherry is preferable to richer, sweeter sherries. Dry and sweet vermouths are served separately, mixed together, or the former is mixed with gin to make a Martini cocktail. Cocktails are usually based on gin mixed with other aperitifs. A pink gin merely requires the addition of a few drops of Angostura bitters. Have ready a supply of ice and slices of lemon in case guests prefer gin and tonic. The host usually deals with pre-dinner drinks to allow the hostess time to see to the food. Sometimes sherry is served with soup and the first wine offered should be a dry white to accompany the hors d'oeuvre and fish courses. A medium dry white or rosé goes well with poultry, veal, or made-up dishes in a white sauce. Red wine is appropriate with red meat or game, and with cheese. A sweet white wine to go with dessert is not obligatory as people no longer expect a vast succession of wines, although it is still usual to offer brandy or liqueurs with coffee.

Other drinks: If you have decided not to serve alcohol with the meal, but it does call for some kind of drink to accompany it, this need not be tea, coffee or plain tap water. Home-made lemonade is delicious, especially at lunch time. Lemons go much further if you steep the squeezed lemon halves in boiling water until this becomes cold. Strain and add to the lemonade. Fizzy drinks always look and taste better if served chilled. Pour them out at the last moment, pop in a cube or two of ice and a slice of lemon and serve in tall glasses with a straw. Iced black tea and coffee are refreshingly different. Add a scoop of vanilla ice cream, or a float of cream to the surface of the coffee, and a slice of lemon or a sprig of mint to the tea.

To end a gala dinner party on the right note, offer Gaelic coffee instead of the more usual coffee and liqueurs. Warm wine glasses of the Paris goblet shape, pour in a small measure of whisky, add a teaspoon of sugar and stir well. Fill the glasses two-thirds full with strong hot black coffee and pour in lightly-whipped cream over the back of a teaspoon. The two layers should remain separate. Sip the coffee through the cream.

CARVING

The most important piece of equipment for carving is a long, sharp knife. Armed with this, a two-pronged fork with a handguard and, possibly a second shorter knife, and an ordinary table fork, you should find that a joint of meat will present no difficulty.

Here is a guide showing directions of main cut, rather than the carving position. The fork is used to hold the meat firm against the action of the knife, and the handguard is essential in case the knife slips towards your hand.

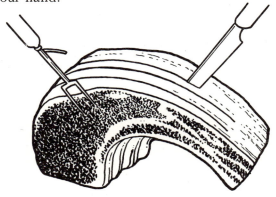

Roast Rib of Beef: Place joint upright on a dish, supporting it with the fork, rib side on the left. Cut the first slice down from the outside edge furthest away from you to the rib bone. Remove with the aid of a second fork. Continue carving parallel slices, and if necessary release by sliding knife at right angles just above and close to the bone.

Round of Beef: Not so easy to carve as it would appear, unless placed flat on a spiked carving dish. Anchor the joint firmly with the carving fork, then use a very sharp knife, cutting against the support of the fork. Cut a thick slice from the top of the joint, leaving it smooth, then carve thin slices.

Sirloin of Beef: Place joint on its side, undercut uppermost. Support with the fork and cut slices through to the bone. Place joint flat on dish and carve down close to the bone, to release the slices. Reverse process to carve the uppercut of the joint.

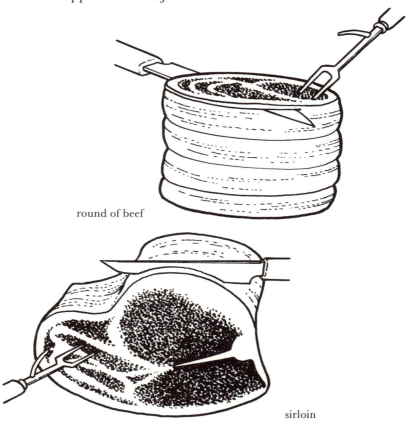

round of beef

sirloin

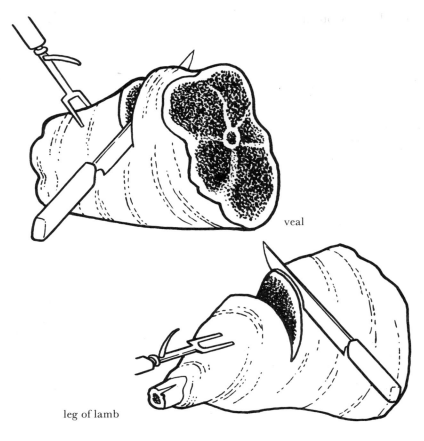

veal

leg of lamb

Veal Top of Leg: Place joint on its side, supporting with the carving fork. Make V-cut through to the bone and carve slices from each side of the cut. Turn the joint over and carve the other side in the same way.
Leg of Lamb: Place leg so that the thick meaty section is facing you. Insert fork in the large end of the leg and cut two or three slices, lengthwise, from the thin side of the leg (the side away from you). Turn joint to stand on the surface just cut. Insert fork into the meaty section which should now be on top. Starting at the shank end (the narrow end) cut thin slices down to the large leg bone. With fork still in place run knife along leg bone to release the slices. More slices can now be cut from the underside.

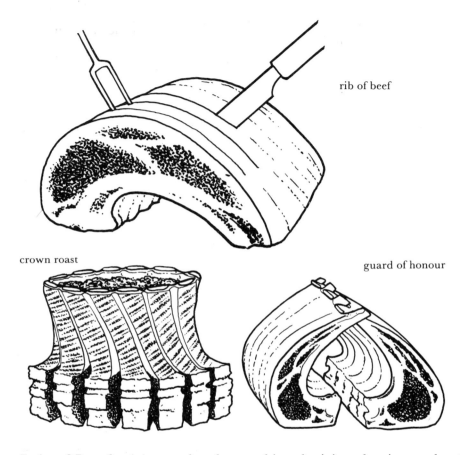

rib of beef

crown roast

guard of honour

Loin of Lamb: Ask your butcher to chine the joint, that is saw the backbone through lengthwise. Holding the joint steady with the carving fork, cut down between the bones and serve as chops. A loin can be completely boned by the butcher, stuffed and carved as a round of beef.

Best End of Neck: Have your butcher prepare and sew together two best ends to make a crown roast, bones outwards. Fill the centre with stuffing, and carve between the rib bones, dividing the meat into cutlets each with a portion of stuffing. Alternatively, get the butcher to prepare a guard of honour; the two best ends are placed face to face, bone side inwards, and the trimmed cutlet bones interlaced alternately, to retain the best ends in a standing position.

Shoulder of Lamb: Raise joint from dish with the carving fork and cut slices parallel to the face of the meat. Lay joint down again and carve meat on either side of the blade bone and knuckle end.

Leg of Pork: Holding joint down with carving fork, carry knife right through the crackling down to the bone, in the same way as for leg of lamb. Remove some of the crackling if this makes carving easier, and break up on the plate.

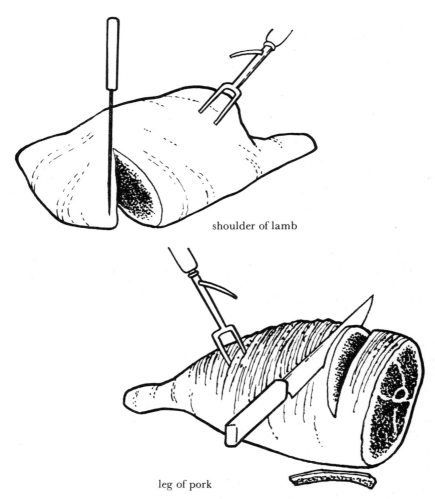

shoulder of lamb

leg of pork

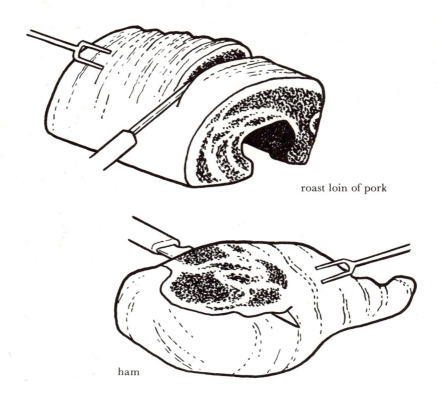

roast loin of pork

ham

Loin of Pork: Crackling should be scored in diamond shapes so that it divides easily into small portions. Remove some crackling before carving and carve as for loin of lamb.

Whole Ham: Place on the dish so that the bone end is at your right. Cut two or three slices from the thin side of the ham, then turn to stand on the surface just cut. Remove a small wedge from the bone end and, with the carving fork steadying the ham, cut thin horizontal slices starting from the wedge. Then run knife along the leg bone to release the slices. For more slices, turn ham back to first position and cut at right angles to the bone.

Opposite A table set with bronze cutlery and goblets gives a beautiful golden glow to the whole setting.

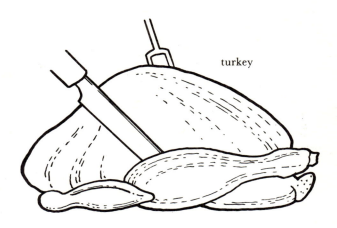

turkey

Turkey and other Poultry: Place bird with legs to the right. Insert fork just below the breast, being careful not to puncture the breast itself. Slice thigh and leg from the body. Remove to a separate plate to carve later. Pull wing from body as far as possible, work knife through the joint, twist from body and remove. Now carve thin slices parallel to the breast bone along the breast meat. Finally separate the leg from the thigh and cut long thin slices from it with your second shorter knife.

HOW TO COPE WITH A FORMAL DINNER PARTY

Today's style of entertaining, even on formal occasions, is much more relaxed and easy-going than it used to be. Nevertheless, there are certain accepted rules which you will want to follow, particularly for some special occasion which entails seating a large party. Serving several courses to a number of people can be quite a complicated affair. Without careful planning, smooth progress of the meal might be held up, especially if the host and hostess are managing without outside help.

Following these general rules will ensure that your big dinner party is a pleasant and successful social occasion.

Lay the table well in advance so that you can reserve all your efforts for tasks which must be left until after the party has begun. Ensure that there are at least two condiment sets if there are more than four people

Left A formal dinner is enhanced by an elegant room, but with careful planning, any hostess can make her dinner party a successful occasion.

seated. The same rule applies to butter dishes, and baskets of rolls or bread. Remind the host to see to the wine so that it is at the correct temperature when needed.

Arrange beforehand which serving responsibilities will be undertaken by the host and which by the hostess. Probably the host will be responsible for dispensing pre-dinner drinks; opening, preparing and pouring the wine. The hostess will take care of the food, apart from carving at table, which is another task traditionally undertaken by the man. If coping single-handed, the hostess brings in and removes each course in turn, with tactful help in clearing the table by the host.

Wine service

If the host pours, he will serve the ladies first, ending with the hostess, then the men, ending with himself, pouring from the right of the table setting. If a maid pours, she will serve all the guests in turn, beginning with the most important lady. The glasses will be arranged in the order they are to be used, ranging outwards from the guest's right hand. This reverses the procedure for the setting of cutlery, which is used from the outside of both sides of the table setting inwards, beginning with one odd piece on the right hand if necessary (such as the soup spoon). It is no longer usual, even if a maid is serving, to offer a host the ritual opportunity to taste a small sample of each wine. As each course finishes, either the maid or the host himself will pour wine for the next course. This often bridges the gap while guests are waiting for the next course. At the end of the meal, the host should offer a choice of brandy or liqueurs and he or the maid will bring in a tray with a selection of bottles, from which he will pour, and suitable glasses. If the dinner is very formal it might end by serving port from a decanter to 'men only'; while the women depart to take coffee in another room, and be joined by the male members of the party later. Glasses for port should be set only when dessert is served, and the other wine glasses removed. The decanter of port is passed from hand to hand always to the left, and never across the table.

Wine serving hints

Since wine stains table linen and clothes, great care must be taken not to spill any drops while pouring it. Swathe a clean folded napkin round the neck of the bottle and give the bottle a smooth quarter turn as you remove it from the glass after pouring. Be careful not to disturb sediment in red wine when doing this, but such a problem can always be avoided by decanting the wine before serving. If the host notices a fragment of cork in a guest's glass, he should unobtrusively remove the glass and if necessary exchange it with his own.

Service of food

All service is from the left, including the removal of plates. If the hostess has to manage without help in serving, it is best to begin the meal with an hors d'oeuvre already laid, or with soup plates filled and set on the table on service plates before the guests sit down.

Nowadays, it is unlikely that more than one person would be available to help serve at table, or to work behind the scenes in the kitchen. If a maid is employed, she would serve the first course after the party is seated, and then the wine (unless the host has decided to do this himself). It is now customary for side plates to be set even on very formal occasions, and unless a maid offers a basket of rolls or bread at the beginning of the meal to each guest in turn, bread baskets should be placed on the table. Guests will then serve themselves with bread and butter throughout the meal.

When the first course is finished, the hors d'oeuvres or soup plates, and any accompaniments, should be removed with their service plates by the maid or hostess. If there is a second course before the main course, it should not have accompanying vegetables which require separate service, as this is much too complicated for a hostess to deal with at home. The plates should be handed round with the course fully served out on each plate. Smooth transition from the first to second courses requires either the hostess to prepare the plates and the maid to pass them round, or if there is a helper in the kitchen she can prepare the plates and the hostess will pass them. Where there is no helper at all, the host will probably assist the hostess both to clear and serve, and take the opportunity of getting up from the table to refill wine glasses or pour the second wine.

It is usual to serve vegetables separately from the main course, although quite often the second course is omitted. Many people find a three-course dinner (perhaps followed by both cheese and dessert) more than adequate. Now that the provision of an interesting cheese board is often a feature of the meal, the menu would be too extended if it included more than either soup or hors d'oeuvre, followed by a main course, followed by a sweet, ending with cheese or dessert, or possibly both.

There are two ways to deal with the service of a hot main course with separate vegetables. Either the hostess or a helper serves out portions complete with vegetables for each guest in the kitchen and these are carried round; or plates with the main course are put in front of the guests and vegetable dishes and sauce-boats are placed on the table to be passed round. Remember, it is important to speed up service before the food becomes cold, as guests are reluctant to begin eating before everyone has been served, even if invited to do so. Service is very slow if a maid carries round vegetable dishes offering them to each guest, or serves each guest in turn, and this should be avoided. It is not usual at formal dinners to offer second helpings.

If a second wine is served at the beginning of the main course it should be poured either by the host or by the maid. The glasses already used are not removed. This is for the convenience of guests who prefer to drink white wine throughout the meal. The plates and accompaniments of this course will be removed in the same way as before, also the the condiments. Unless there is a beautifully decorated sweet for guests to admire which the hostess can speedily serve out into dessert dishes or on to small plates at table, individual portions are more conveniently served directly from the kitchen. These dishes and such items as a cream jug or sugar sifter brought in for the sweet will be removed at the same time. The cheese tray will then be circulated for which guests can use their side plates if china is in short supply.

When port is not served, the coffee tray may be brought to the table, after the cheeseboard has been cleared, and dessert offered. When there is no dessert or fruit, delicate chocolate mints or *petits four* are often handed with coffee. The hostess usually pours the coffee although it may be handed round quite informally by the guests themselves. Fresh coffee should be available in reserve if the gentlemen are to 'join the ladies' after enjoying their port.

It is helpful to observe how successive courses are served at a formal dinner in hotel or restaurant, even though you cannot do exactly the same at home. To sum up, the entire meal can be served by the host and hostess alone without problems, providing they arrange beforehand who undertakes each duty and in what order; and if a helper is employed she must also be quite clear about which duties will be hers.

Part 4
Caring for your table-layout treasures

Every item connected with setting the table for a meal requires regular cleaning and·maintenance even if not washing after each use. Stained linen, or scratched cutlery for instance, detract from the charm of a well-planned table layout, so avoid damage as far as possible and maintain your prize possessions carefully.

Today, there are many branded stain removers and cleaners which frequently appear to work miracles. But sometimes old methods succeed when they fail, so some hints given here are ones your grandmother might have used. Liquid detergent which produces a foamy solution can be used as an alternative to soapy water wherever this is mentioned.

TABLE SURFACES AND CHAIRS

Wood

With the exception of whitewood, all wooden furniture has been given a final surface treatment by the manufacturer. That is why it is important to know what the material is when you buy and if possible obtain advice on how it should be cared for. If this original finish is to keep its good looks, it needs a certain amount of regular attention but this depends on the kind of finish involved. Day-to-day care should be kept to dusting; cleaning and/or polishing should be done weekly. (Some surfaces require no polishing.) This gives a better result than a daily application of polish. It is a fallacy that furniture should be polished to 'feed the wood'. It is important to remove dirt thoroughly to prevent a patina of dirt, mixed with polish, from building up. Get into the habit of using heat-proof mats on tables which need them and make sure the mats give effective protection.

Wax polish

Furniture that has been wax-polished really does need elbow grease to bring it up. A good furniture wax can be used occasionally, but sparingly, because the solvent in the polish softens the basic wax leaving a smeary surface. So always use the minimum and buff well. Teak and 'oiled' woods need a few drops of teak oil every 3–4 months.

French polish

The high gloss of a French polish should last for years if handled carefully. Polish occasionally with a little beeswax-based furniture cream and remove any build-up of wax with a mixture of 1 part vinegar to 8 parts water. Remove sticky marks with a little warm soapy water, dry thoroughly afterwards. Heat marks should disappear if rubbed with linseed oil or olive oil and cigarette ash or cigar ash (these mild abrasives could be added to the oil without harm). Old or worn French polish is best removed and a new surface applied professionally although DIY kits are available.

Plastic finishes

Modern clear 'plastic' finishes protect furniture well against dust, grease and grime. A gloss finish is best maintained with the occasional use of a cleaning and polishing liquid; a matt finish should be wiped lightly with a moist chamois leather. Too much polishing on matt surfaces will destroy the matt effect, causing an ugly 'bloom'. Once you begin using polish you may find that it becomes a regular chore.

Laminates

Laminates require nothing beyond a wipe with a damp cloth. If you do use a little household cleaner be sure to rinse all traces away with a clean damp cloth. Drying with a soft cloth prevents smearing.

Eggshell paint

This should be washed over with warm water and a mild detergent. A small amount of white furniture cream used occasionally will improve the surface.

Bamboo

To clean bamboo wipe with a damp cloth and pat dry with a soft absorbent cloth. If badly soiled, add a tablespoon of common salt to every 500ml/1 pint of water and apply with a soft brush. Wipe dry with a soft cloth, then rub the surface with a piece of velvet soaked in linseed oil. Leave for an hour or so, then polish with a soft cloth.

Canework and rush

Canework should be vacuum-dusted using a rubber upholstery nozzle. Old and grubby cane can be cleaned using a soft brush and a *minimum* of warm, slightly soapy water. Do small sections at a time; rinse away any soap traces with a clean damp cloth and pat dry with a colourfast towel. Rush seating should be similarly vacuumed. Avoid using water unless advised otherwise when purchasing.

Most modern bamboo, cane and rushwork is 'sealed' during manufacturing stages with chemical agents. Be extra careful to make a permanent note of the furniture maker's cleaning instructions and if in doubt consult a good furniture store.

Marble

Marble can be cleaned by lightly scouring with powdered borax and then washing with plain warm water. When this treatment is not effective a solution of oxalic acid can be applied. Proprietary cleaners are also available.

Glass and mirror surfaces

Glass table tops if very dirty should first be rubbed with damp crumpled newspaper. Then use a damp chamois leather, polishing after with a dry one. You may also use a special window cleaning preparation or general household cleaner, but do watch for overpowering perfumes. Put on with absorbent paper or cloth and polish off with a clean rag.

Mirrored surfaces may be cleaned with the same proprietary cleaners as glass. Alternatively use a soft cloth with methylated spirit.

Steel and chrome

Tubular steel is cleaned with a modern 'sparkle' polish and chrome with a proprietary chrome cleaner, following the maker's instructions.

Upholstery

Upholstery should be brushed or vacuumed regularly and shampooed occasionally with a branded cleaner. Take care not to overwet the fabric and aid drying by opening windows or switching on a fan heater. Avoid spraying polish on to chair upholstery by applying to wood parts with a cloth. Grease marks respond to a grease solvent or to a hot iron and blotting paper. Place the paper over the mark and iron gently. (This technique may also be used with carpets.)

Vinyl and plastic materials should be regularly wiped with a damp, soapy cloth. Wipe away any soap traces with a clean damp cloth and buff away moisture drops with a soft rag.

The beauty of real leather seat covers can be preserved by the same treatment. Treat occasionally with light application of 'hide-food' – branded preparations are available.

Dealing with disasters

The golden rule is treat as soon as possible without turning a party into a panic. White heat marks that have not penetrated too deeply should be gently rubbed with a soft cloth dipped in camphorated oil. Treat a small part at a time and wipe away any surplus oil. Wax and polish in the normal way.

Persistent marks can be camouflaged by a special wood dye (following the manufacturer's instructions); burns that have penetrated the surface may mean stripping and re-polishing. A deep burn that has destroyed the wood can only be masked by staining and polishing.

Hot grease is ideally removed at once with soft paper. If set, lift off with a blunt knife. Use the same method for melted candle wax. Polish well.

There are various methods of removing bad water marks such as glass rings. One method is to soak very fine steel wool in liquid furniture cream and polish hard over the mark. This may be successful, but if not hold a lighted match in one hand over the mark to warm the surface, taking care not to burn the surface. With the other hand polish the mark very hard with a slightly tinted furniture cream or dye. When the mark has nearly disappeared, wax and polish in the usual way. Ordinary iodine is useful to touch up scratches on dark woods. Make a trial application first on a small area and if the result is too dark dilute it with alcohol. For lighter woods, rub the scratch with a fresh shelled and halved Brazil nut.

TABLE-CLOTHS AND NAPKINS

Care of table linens will depend on the materials from which they are made. By and large, synthetics require less attention than most pure cottons and linens, or mixtures of natural and man-made fibres. But the beauty of starched cloths and napkins is often well worth the effort involved in laundering and ironing them.

Synthetic Fabrics

Synthetic fabrics should be washed in accordance with maker's directions but as a general rule they may be either machine-washed on the appropriate programme or hand-washed in warm water. Hand-washed articles may be pre-soaked but should not be wrung out, simply drip-dried. Usually ironing is not necessary, although some fibres can be lightly pressed with a warm iron if liked. Synthetic fabrics should not be starched.

Natural Fibres

Natural fibres such as cotton and linen may be machine-washed delicate hand woven linens, embroidery or lace-worked articles should be placed inside an old pillow case); but many people prefer to hand-wash. Pre-wash soaking in tepid water for about half an hour will loosen small particles of grime and any marks or stains. Whites are washed in very hot water and boiled every few washes to retain whiteness. Coloured linens should be tested for colour fastness by ironing between pieces of cotton. Fast colours can then be washed in cooler water. Cotton organdie is similarly treated. All natural fibres, except seersuckers and similar 'bubble' materials, may be starched (see below).

Thorough rinsing in clean water will help to keep your table linen gleaming and fresh. Greying linens may be brightened up with good old-fashioned blueing agents. These come in powder or liquid form, and it is essential to dissolve thoroughly otherwise spotting will occur. Articles should be loosly immersed and evenly wetted in the solution. If cloth is over-blued a further rinse in warm water with a splash of white vinegar will adjust the tint.

Ironing and folding table linens

All table linen, especially if starched, needs to be correctly folded: then it will store without creasing and those odd diamond shaped folds which seem to appear by magic will be an irritation of the past. Only starched napkins can be folded into ornamental shapes that stay put.

Starching

With powder starches that dissolve in water, table linens are starched wet immediately following washing/rinsing. If necessary fold each item neatly and dip one at a time. Hang out to dry keeping as flat as possible. Aerosol starches should be evenly sprayed on to damp linen. Starching is easier to iron while still damp. If it does over-dry, damp-down by sprinkling with water, folding and rolling into a small parcel. Leave for about an hour. Always iron from the centre out, gently pulling the napkins and cloths into shape: they should have good square corners and really straight edges.

Table mats

Iron starched table mats flat on both sides, teasing out with your fingers fringed edges that have become tangles. They may also need some persuasive stretching to become completely square again.

Embroidery

Embroidery on cloths and napkins should be pressed face down onto a soft cloth or towel to restore its beauty. The plain parts are first ironed and folded as above.

Lace

Cotton lace should be ironed from the centre out being gently pulled into shape. Delicate lace should be protected between sheets of tissue paper.

CHINA

Bone china and porcelain

Take care when washing up to use warm soapy water with the detergent liquid well dissolved. Too hot water or neat detergent poured onto the china will in time spoil both colour and glaze. Rinse in clean warm water and drain dry and polish with a soft cloth, or wipe dry as liked. Most china can be placed in a dish washer but where the china is very valuable, it is probably wiser to wash it by hand. This rule certainly applies to china decorated with gold leaf or other precious metal decoration.

Do not put plates into a hot oven or under the grill to warm unless sold as oven-proof.

Stains

Silver stains from cutlery can easily be removed from china by a silver polish. Do not use harsh abrasives as they will remove the glaze. A small amount of salt on a dish cloth will shift tea stains. Alternatively soak in detergent solution.

Fill a badly stained teapot with detergent suds to which has been added a good teaspoon of salt. Allow to stand for one hour, then rinse out thoroughly.

Storing best china

In spite of the fact that cups look very nice on hooks, it is not a good way of storing your best ones, since there is too much weight on delicate handles. If you store valuable plates in piles, protect them from scratching by interleaving with soft tissue or cloth. Allow plenty of space for storing your best china rather than pile it into a small cupboard.

CUTLERY

The best method of caring for all cutlery, whatever it is made from, is to wash and dry immediately after use. In this way all food residues are removed before staining can occur. No cutlery is totally stain-resistant, so do not leave it unwashed, wet or 'in soak' overnight – even in a dish washer. First rinse under cold running water to remove any traces of salt; salt plus hot water can cause staining and pitting. Next wash in clean, warm, soapy water, rinse and dry thoroughly. Use soft dish pads or cloths and tea towels, and never add bleach to the water. Handle each piece separately: cutlery cluttered in a bowl may get scratched.

Drying
Knife blades, nowadays usually made from stainless steel, should not be wiped with an up-and-down movement, but in one direction only from neck to point until all the moisture is removed. This method is best for spoons and forks too.

Stainless steel cutlery
While stainless steel requires very little special attention, the above routine should still be followed. Any stains that do occur are usually due to an accidental application of silver cleaning material or to prolonged contact with acids and minerals – salt, vinegar or even those naturally present in tap water. Steel wool fragments can cause rust marks if carelessly left in contact as can corrosion pitting, although this is only likely to occur in cheap imported pieces. Very hard water can deposit a chalky film and very hot fat or meat juices (and of course direct heat if cutlery is left on a hot plate) can cause stubborn rainbow stains. Most stains that resist ordinary rubbing with a soapy cloth can be corrected with Goddard's stainless steel care.

Horn and wood handles
Cutlery with handles of horn or natural polished wood should not be machine washed, nor even placed bodily into water. Simply hold each piece by the handle and wash only the metal parts. As the handles may become damp, dry each thoroughly as soon as possible. Plastic-finished woods do not need polish, but if plunged in water frequently they become grey and dull.

China and stone-ware
These handles should be washed as china. Certain types of plastic

handles which look like china should not be subjected to the heat of dish washers so note manufacturer's instructions.

Silver and silver plate

Silver and silver plate including EPNS should be washed and dried as above and never in a dish washer. Silver is a comparatively soft metal and no matter what care is taken it is inevitable that small scratches will appear on the polished surface. This results in a less brilliant, but no less attractive, appearance. Tarnishing is easily removed by a good silver polish. 'Long term' polishes are probably the best as they do provide a high degree of protection against subsequent tarnishing. A silver dip is useful for keeping fork prongs and teaspoons immaculate. Silver cleaners should never be allowed into contact with stainless steel knife blades.

Pewter

This is a real easy-care metal, but if tarnished through non-use, the lustre can be restored with silver polish. Otherwise, treat as stainless steel.

Bronze and vermeil

Bronze and vermeil and gilded stainless steel cutlery should be washed as silver and should not tarnish.

Storage

The ideal way to store cutlery is in a canteen. These can be purchased separately from leading stores or can be made by the home handyman. Choose between the open box or cabinet draw type, free-standing or on legs. A plain felt lining and a sectioned insert for convenient stacking will keep cutlery well protected and tidy.

Alternatively use a carry box divided into sections and similarly lined. A piece of loose felt laid over the cutlery will keep dust and damp away. Felts should be softly brushed to keep them clean.

GLASSWARE

Fine glass, particularly valuable crystal, should be washed by hand and not in a dish washer. Use a plastic bowl or a rubber mat in the sink and warm, not hot, soapy water with a soft cloth or sponge. Pressed or engraved patterns can be cleaned with a soft brush. Glasses used for milk or alcoholic beverages should be pre-rinsed in cold water. Wash one glass at a time to prevent chipping and rinse in plain warm water. Some people like to add a splash of vinegar to the rinsing water to remove all soap or detergent traces. Drain on a rubber mat or plastic-coated drainer or on a folded towel. When clearing up after a party, take a tip from the publicans and cover trays with cloths or kitchen paper, leaving glasses to drain whilst you do other jobs. In an hour or so they will be ready to polish with a soft, non-fluffy cloth.

Stains

Obstinate marks on glass are dissolved by soaking the glass for 24 hours in a strong solution of household detergent and water or rubbing very carefully with a cleaning powder. For lime deposits use tea leaves soaked in vinegar. If the problem is excessive caking on the inside of a bottle or decanter the addition of a little silver sand will be helpful. Swirl round vigorously before pouring it out.

Stuck glasses and stoppers

When glasses stick together do not attempt to pry them apart. Pour cold water on the inner glass and hold the outer one in warm water. Stoppers which stick can eventually be removed from decanters by rubbing a little cooking oil around the joint and leaving in a warm place. But a certain amount of patience may be needed.

Storage

Glasses not in regular use can be packed away safely in cardboard boxes. Wrap glasses individually in tissue paper or newspaper and lay side by side in alternative rows, rims to bases, with layers separated by several sheets of paper. Alternatively use strong scissors and make proper cardboard box dividers or save the ones used in cases of wine for this purpose. They fold flat when not required. Glasses that have been stored should always be washed before use. At first glance they may look clean, but are probably dusty or at best, less than sparkling.

Index